P

Know Your Own Mind

James Greene is a psychologist whose research and professional interests encompass psychological assessment. While studying for his masters degree in psychology, he became interested in the assessment and development of human potential. He has since carried out research in ability testing and has advised companies on this topic. Together with David Lewis, he has written several popular books aimed at helping readers to find out more about themselves and to make the most of this knowledge. In addition to a busy writing schedule, he is presently carrying out research with children on new methods of educational diagnosis and self-improvement. He also provides a consultancy service to industry on techniques of assessment of candidates for employment and promotion, and methods of making the best use of company trainees' talents.

David Lewis was born in London in 1948. Educated in France, Britain and America, he holds a first class honours degree in psychology and postgraduate qualifications in psychometrics. After studying medicine he worked in journalism for a number of years before returning to academic studies. His special area of interest is the effect of emotional responses on intellectual performance, and he is founder of Children Unlimited, an organization which teaches parents how to help their children learn more successfully. A lecturer, broadcaster, and the author of more than twelve books on social and psychological subjects, his first book, *Most Unnatural: An Inquiry into the Stafford Case* (Penguin 1970) made legal history by leading to the retrial of two men serving life sentences for murder. His other books include *The Secret Language of Your Child, How to be a Gifted Parent, You Can Teach Your Child Intelligence* and *Thinking Better* (with James Greene). He is currently engaged in a Medical Research Council funded study at the University of Sussex.

KNOW YOUR OWN MIND

YOUR HIDDEN TALENTS
SCIENTIFICALLY REVEALED

James Greene and David Lewis

PENGUIN BOOKS

PENGUIN BOOKS

Published by the Penguin Group
27 Wrights Lane, London W8 5TZ, England
Viking Penguin Inc., 40 West 23rd Street, New York, New York 10010, USA
Penguin Books Australia Ltd, Ringwood, Victoria, Australia
Penguin Books Canada Ltd, 2801 John Street, Markham, Ontario, Canada L3R 1B4
Penguin Books (NZ) Ltd, 182–190 Wairau Road, Auckland 10, New Zealand

Penguin Books Ltd, Registered Offices: Harmondsworth, Middlesex, England

First published 1983
Reprinted 1984, 1985, 1987, 1988

Made and printed in Great Britain by
Hazell Watson & Viney Limited
Member of BPCC plc
Aylesbury Bucks
Set in Linotron Plantin by
Rowland Phototypesetting Ltd
Bury St Edmunds, Suffolk

CONTENTS

Introduction 7

How To Use This Book 10

ASSESSMENT ONE 13

ASSESSMENT TWO 31

ASSESSMENT THREE 42

ASSESSMENT FOUR 55

ASSESSMENT FIVE 69

ASSESSMENT SIX 83

ASSESSMENT SEVEN 93

ASSESSMENT EIGHT 108

ASSESSMENT NINE 120

YOUR HIDDEN TALENTS IN ACTION 132

Index 142

INTRODUCTION

'Knowledge itself is power', wrote Francis Bacon. Certainly, when it comes to knowing about our own aptitudes and discovering our hidden talents, few would deny the truth of that statement. It is only by gaining such self-knowledge that we can realize our full intellectual potential.

The purpose of this book is to provide that vital insight. By working through the assessments which follow, you will be able to:

- identify the type of thinking for which your brain is best suited;
- discover your capacity for logical reasoning and scientific deduction;
- explore your artistic talents;
- find out whether or not you have a flair for languages and, if so, which you could learn most easily;
- assess your powers of co-ordination to see if you possess the level of skill needed for many jobs and hobbies;
- investigate your social intelligence and ability to express yourself effectively;
- pinpoint the kind of career and type of leisure activity which you should be able to do best and enjoy the most.

Everybody hopes to find a job well-suited to his or her special aptitudes. Yet very few people understand how to assess those aptitudes effectively. As a result, many go into employment for which they are ill-suited, and so end up frustrated, bored or over-stressed. Their intellectual powers lie dormant instead of being properly employed to bring them the best chances for success and fulfilment.

This lack of self-knowledge has serious implications both for individuals and for society. Studies have shown that at least one-third of the working population in Britain and the United States are seriously dissatisfied with their jobs. They either complain that the work is beyond their capabilities, or is insufficiently stimulating. Those who find the going too tough express concern because they cannot master important concepts in the work or use their minds in the right way to achieve important goals in that particular activity. On the other hand, they may find the demands being made on their mind are all too trivial; boredom and lack of interest rapidly set in because the work is *too easy*, the tasks far too readily handled, the stimulation their minds demand almost totally absent.

In some cases, of course, these people did not really want a particular job but were obliged to take it because nothing else was available at the time. In the majority of instances, however, research has shown that those unhappy and underachieving workers went into their jobs quite voluntarily.

'I didn't really know what I wanted to do,' one unhappy young office worker told us. 'I still don't, and this is my third job in two years. I always seem to be a square peg in a round hole.'

A similar story is told by many of those once eager mature students who, around October each year, sign up for an evening course at some college of higher education. They begin their studies with great determination and enthusiasm, certain that they have both a genuine interest in, and a real aptitude for, a particular course of study. As the weeks pass, however, more and more empty spaces appear at the desks as students begin to drop out of the class. What had been approached so eagerly only a short time earlier has now been abandoned as either insufficiently stimulating, too difficult or just not what was wanted. Records of evening institutes in Britain and the United States reveal that the drop-out rate is a staggering 58% – that is, more than half of those eager adults who queued to sign up for a class never complete the course.

At a more personal level, we can see the same sort of failure rate when it comes to hobbies in the home. Go into almost any house in the land and you will find evidence of discarded leisure pursuits, often involving hundreds of pounds' worth of equipment, gathering dust in cupboards and attics: language courses abandoned by the third cassette – craft equipment, from potter's wheels to oil-painting sets, barely used – home tuition courses of every kind, from electronic kits to car maintenance manuals, purchased with enthusiasm then set aside without further thought before a couple of months have passed.

How can we explain such widespread squandering of time and money, effort and interest? Why should high hopes become transformed so rapidly into loss of interest, and determination give way so quickly to indifference?

The simple truth is that most people often don't really know their own mind. They fail to understand their mental strengths and weaknesses and so get attracted by a career, a training course or a leisure activity for which they are ill-equipped to cope intellectually. While the term 'hidden talents' is something of a cliché, it remains a fact that, for many people, some of their most useful talents will always remain hidden from view.

The hidden talents which most of us need to know far more about are called aptitudes by psychologists. This simply means a readiness to acquire a certain skill or master a particular subject, and must be distinguished from the idea of abilities, which describe an already established level of expertise in some particular activity. Usually, of course, the first step towards developing an ability is recognizing that an aptitude exists.

Perhaps what we have said so far strikes a familiar chord. If you have experienced similar frustrations or dissatisfactions in work or at play, then you will know exactly what we mean. But how can you tell whether you do have hidden talents, aptitudes for activities which you have never discovered? Well, the mere fact that you were interested enough to read this book suggests that you do, indeed, possess a so far unexploited, or underexploited, talent.

While carrying out the researches on which our assessments are based, we asked people from all walks of life to carry out three tasks. First, they were requested to rate themselves on various aptitudes, to carry out a highly subjective evaluation of their talents for certain activities. Then we inquired whether they would be interested in doing a series of tests that would enable them to evaluate those same aptitudes scientifically. Finally they carried out the assessments which you will find in the book.

The results were fascinating. We discovered that the stronger their interest in testing their aptitudes objectively, the more likely it was that hidden talents did indeed exist. We also found that those same people tended to rate their talents in these areas far more negatively than the objective assessment. They evaluated a particular aptitude as being fairly slight when the tests revealed their talent to be above average. In other words, they had little idea of their own potential. They did not really know their own minds.

As a result of this study we can say with some confidence that you would not have been attracted to a book like this unless you felt, however vaguely, that you were not making the best use of your brain; that the things you turned your mind to in the past did not exploit your mental skills to the full.

The assessments in this book have been specially developed to provide a fast, reliable identification of aptitudes in all major areas of intellectual endeavour, from the kind of thinking essential to success in mathematics and science, to artistic, mechanical and social skills.

Reading and using this book should, therefore, prove the first step to alleviating any feelings of dissatisfaction, while at the same time setting you on the right road to greater accomplishment and success. You are going to investigate the workings of your mind so as to come to a fuller understanding of your major aptitudes. You will also learn how these talents can be put to work in the most effective manner, whether you are trying to choose a career, embark on a course of further education or select a leisure activity that will give lasting pleasure.

HOW TO USE THIS BOOK

To get the best out of our book you should follow the instructions given below.

1   Do not try to complete all the assessments at one sitting. Attempting this would not only prove extremely tiring but actually counter-productive. In order to assess an aptitude accurately, you need to approach the test with a fresh mind. At the start of each test you will find detailed instructions on how to take that assessment, the time required and the materials needed. Work through the book over a period of two or three weeks in order to give yourself time to reflect on the results of each assessment and so savour the experience of self-discovery.

2   It is essential that you complete each test before reading the rest of the chapter. This is necessary for two important reasons. First of all, the answers to each assessment are provided immediately after the questions – and prior knowledge of these would obviously invalidate the test. Second, we often do not tell you exactly which aptitude a particular test is assessing until after you have attempted the questions. We have done this deliberately, because most adults have firmly established beliefs about the things they can and cannot accomplish. From childhood onwards we build up a mental image of ourselves and our capacity for coping with particular kinds of challenge or succeeding in certain types of task. For example, you often hear people assure you: 'I'm hopeless at maths,' or, 'I could never learn a language.' They will confess their utter helplessness when confronted by a mechanical task, or refuse to accept that they might be able to reason scientifically. These attitudes, usually held for many years and firmly believed, influence an individual's performance adversely when he or she is trying to tackle any task that is felt to be beyond them. This creates a self-fulfilling prophecy of failure, since the low score which is almost inevitably obtained serves to increase their conviction that they have no aptitude for a particular activity. To try and avoid such prejudgments, we have not identified any of the assessments prior to their being taken. In some instances, of course, you are bound to have a good idea of the type of aptitude being assessed. This is unavoidable because no valid assessment could be disguised to the extent that you remained

completely in the dark while working through it. But try to approach each with a completely neutral attitude and do not always take the assessments at their face value. They may not, necessarily, be assessing what you believe them to be while you are working through the problems. We have arranged the assessments in such a way that contrasting mental aptitudes are explored in turn. This should make it more stimulating for you to follow the book in chapter order. But, if you wish to tackle the tests in a different sequence, then feel perfectly free to do so.

3 For much the same reason, you should avoid the temptation of looking at the final chapter until you have completed all the assessments. In this chapter we will be describing how you can create a mental profile which should help you discover the kinds of career most suited to your own particular talents.

4 Some of the tests have to be completed within a specific period of time. This means you should work with a stop-watch or an ordinary watch with a clear face, positioned so that it can easily be seen while you work on the assessment. Be sure to avoid the temptation to carry on with the questions after the specified time – as this will, of course, completely invalidate the results.

Other tests do not have a time limit, but you will be asked to note how long it takes you to complete them. Here the procedure is to write down the exact time you start and finish the test. This type of assessment is short and you will need to time them to the nearest second, so a stop-watch or a timepiece which allows easy readout of the seconds is essential.

Finally, there are tests which have no time factor to consider. Here you can work as long as you wish; but these assessments should always be completed in one sitting, since you will find it very hard to get back into the test if you start again after a lengthy break. This loss of concentration could undermine your performance and so lead to a lower score than would otherwise have been achieved. All the tests have clear directions as to the time factor involved.

5 Some assessments have to be done by working directly on the charts or designs contained in the book. You should avoid marking the pages (especially if you have borrowed the book from a library), both for your own sake and for that of anybody else who may want to take the same tests. In your own case you might care to take some of the tests again, after an interval of several months, to identify any changes which may have occurred in the interim. The best way to get around this problem is to have somebody else make photocopies for you, and then write your answers on these. In most cases it is unwise to do the photocopying yourself, as this may give you prior knowledge of the questions – and this could invalidate the results. The tests where this is necessary will be clearly indicated.

6   Finally, please do not feel upset or worried if you get low marks on some of the assessments. None of them is a *test of intelligence*, and you certainly should not be concerned if a few low scores emerge; indeed, it is quite likely that some tests will produce fairly low marks, while on others you may well obtain an above-average result. This is because we are going to assess the broad spectrum of your mental aptitudes, and everyone's pattern of talents is unique. In some cases we will be providing charts to show you where you stand on a certain aptitude in comparison with the rest of the population. This has been done because, in our experience, many people are curious to know how their own aptitudes compare with those of others. Two points should, however, be borne in mind about these comparisons. First, the standardiza-tion samples we used in arriving at our estimates were relatively small and are only intended to give both you and us a general idea of how people score on a particular assessment. Second, you have to appreciate that there is no practical significance in knowing where you stand in relation to the rest of the population on a certain aptitude. All that matters is your own *pattern of individual aptitudes*. It is this which reveals your intellectual strengths or weaknesses and suggests how you might use your hidden talents to best effect.

ASSESSMENT ONE

In this assessment, both the time taken and the number of errors made contribute to the final score, so it is important to work through the items as quickly and as accurately as possible.

Unless otherwise instructed, we advise you to *ignore* any mistakes you notice while working through the problems. Additional marks gained for accuracy are unlikely to compensate for those lost through the extra time taken. May we repeat that, since you will be working directly on the test forms, the only way to avoid marking the book is to have photocopies made of the material. Clearly, this is essential if you have borrowed your copy from a library; but it is likely to be helpful even if the book is your own property. Many people find it interesting and informative to take the same test again after an interval of several months, to check whether the various aptitudes have increased, declined or remained constant during the intervening period. If you do have copies made, be careful not to look at the test items; the best way is to have a friend make the copies for you. In order to provide an accurate and reliable guide to your true ability, it is essential that this test – like all the others in the book – be taken without prior knowledge of the questions.

HOW TO TAKE THIS TEST

Although there is no time limit on this particular test, you *will* need to make a note of how long it takes you to complete each of the sections. Since accurate measurements are required, you should use a timepiece which indicates seconds or, better still, a stop-watch.

The test is divided into four sections; all four should be completed at one sitting, taking a short break between each. Read the instructions which follow carefully, and check with the notes at the beginning of each section to ensure that you fully understand what is required of you before you start work.

Section One

In this part of the test you will be asked to compare two items and decide whether each pair is different or identical. If you conclude they are *exactly the same*, then write an 'S' on the line which connects them. If you come to the conclusion that they are *different*, then indicate this with the letter 'D'.

For example: George Delaney _D_ George Delany

xsadt _S_ xsadt

$y = 2T$ _D_ $y = 2t$

There are differences in the spelling of the surname and in the use of a capital and lower-case 't'; this means that a 'D' must be written on the connecting lines of the first and last items. The middle pair, however, are identical and so require an 'S'.

Section Two

In this part of the test you will be presented with two sets of symbols. In the first you must cross out any *numbers* which appear; in the second, delete the letter 'O' whenever it occurs in the series.

For example: K G H Ø F T Ø B

Ø U M N H Ø Z Ø

Section Three

The problem here is to decide whether the items have been ranked according to their alphabetical order. If the word is *incorrectly* ranked, then place a tick beside it.

For example:　　∨ _3_ Jones

　　　　　　　　_1_ Claxton

　　　　　　∨ _2_ Southampton

Here Claxton has been correctly ranked at number one because, in an alphabetical listing of those three names, it would clearly come first. However Jones and Southampton have been reversed, since Jones should come second and Southampton third.

Section Four

Here you will be required to place words in one of four categories – Animal, Plant, Machine or Human – and identify that category by placing an 'A', 'P', 'M' or 'H' on the line before each.

For example:　　_P_ rose

　　　　　　　　_H_ girl

　　　　　　　　_A_ dog

　　　　　　　　_M_ aeroplane

When you are ready to begin, note the time and turn over the page (or look at the first photocopy). . .

Place an 'S' on the connecting line if items are the same, a 'D' if they are different.

(1) London Transit _____ London Transport

(2) MacMahon Windows _____ McMahon Windows

(3) integral transforms _____ integral transforms

(4) Lubuce, Lois _____ Lubice, Lois

(5) 3865 _____ 3895

(6) President Wilson _____ President Wilson

(7) vmsdt _____ vmstd

(8) Muriel J. Eddington _____ Muriel J. Eddington

(9) polyethylene polymer _____ polyacetelene polymer

(10) xrobitefz _____ xrobitefz

(11) 598761 _____ 598761

(12) Q44/L769.2 – 5FZ/a* _____ Q44/l769.2 – 5FZ/a*

(13) Professor Wong Hung Fu, PhD _____ Profesor Wong Hung Fu, PhD

(14) 1110100110001 _____ 1110100110001

(15) QWERNDHCG _____ QWERNDHGC

(16) Magnesium + Calcium (Mg^{2+}+Ca^{2+}) ATPase _____ Magneisum + Calcium (Mg^2+Ca^{2+})ATPase

(17) Marvin Geoffreye Trickett _____ Marvin Geoffreye Trickett

(18) J. Harris, BSc, MPhil, MemAS, DipMan, FWeDT _____ J. Harris, BSc, DPhil, MemAS, DipMan, FweDT

(19) XDUSy3ORTgU:Ew _____ XDUSy3ORTgU;Ew

(20) $P(G_n+1) - P(G_n) + P(G_n-1) - (1-1/c)(P(E_n-2))$ _____ $P(G_n+1) - P(G_n) + P(G_n - 1) - (1-1/c)(P(E_n - 2))$

(21) Winnemuktascoga, Mississippi _____ Winnemuktascoga, Mississippi

(22) xpwerii6d7d,00/13 _____ xpwerii6d7d,00/13

(23) 0983746038477 _____ 0983746034877

(24) IHbugdResWcTPi _____ IHbugdResWCtPi

(25) Vladislav Brirzibilszczi _____ Vladislav Brirzibilszczi

(26) RTG/23958694a04/yt39.01 _____ RTG/23958694a0/4yt39.01

(27) 10011011110101101001 _____ 10011011110101101001

(28) 1010 i.u. d-alpha-tocopherol _____ 1010 i.u. d-alpha-tocoferol

(29) rqpirstyxjgbcgte _____ rqpirstyxjgbgcte

(30) Cephalosporins and cephamycins _____ Cephalossporins and cephamycins

Stop and note the time you have taken to complete Section One of the test.

Now take a few minutes' break. When you feel ready to start the next Section, check the time, turn the page and begin . . .

SECTION TWO

PART ONE

Draw a line through all the *numbers* you can find in the list below:

HU8H6SS3B89L3X7CW3GJS6R431HL8Y7BXRG4G2AEW947UXFP9V
QLS5WA6Z89JLDY37Y6GHUD8BV1J6LEB8D6YKI2DT5KFY76LXZ4
PL9KMN7FYEW36VZX2JI1L8RQW72IJGBU9KB3S5CRWQZ7JQ31GY
WHLPB9MN1IF2L93KX3Z7USILT1U5XP6NW89XPQXV7NIZLIT8SW
XPAH4AY9PF3WBNKSR6TILD5J7T1LKCSKEWB6SAL37KA1W7MZXQ
PMNZD46GS8RTWX2J1LFE8CZSA7KDR5PS63MJDTIQESAIIS2BC6

PART TWO

Draw a line through the letter 'O' every time it occurs in the list below:

MNZOHWOFOVXZWLONOOWOTPHOYFNOZXROPOLKYODOKJSOUCOGQU
KTDXOOTXOPIOBFOGCOUQOUCQOUOOUCSOUONJFXEDJOWQOCUQGO
OCGSAOYTUOMOXJDRHSQUCGSAWBJOPOOGYJOGSOGPORESZXOCUQ
UCGQUOGCQUGVUNCQOCFSXRNKJHGQOUIFDSCOZOMOBOHGSZRQCU
JYDXEWASDOYHJOOHVFDXCUQOGFROMONKOZSDFGDSAZERTWOPLOP
COREQUOTAROPEDOSERUTENQTSUOPOPEROTEGOCUOTRUCKUGSQPO
ZSOUOGOGUCQUQUCOQCHTDAKOFDTRDOPHOHOOOHVDSAZETTFDOGO

Note the time taken to complete this Section.

Now take a few minutes' break before starting Section Three. In this you will have to check the list provided to see whether items are correctly numbered according to their alphabetical order. You should place a tick against every item which is incorrectly ranked. (HINT: In this Section only, you will find it to your advantage to change earlier answers if, as you work down the list, you notice mistakes.) When you are ready to start, make a note of the time, turn the page and begin . . .

25	McInnes	39	Smythe
1	Alphonse	21	Jarulska
38	Smith	14	Haalmi
6	Brennan	19	Inigo
42	Zelinski	2	Anderton
12	Gomez	3	Anderson
32	Roebuck	26	Matsuhashi
8	Bunday	27	Perigio
36	Silverman	17	Hansen
4	Becker	13	Gomes
31	Roehampton	20	Jacobi
22	Koumi	44	Kellerman
40	Takahashi	28	Paolo
15	Hampton	10	Chu
16	Hanssen	11	Ginsberg
18	Hodges	29	Quigly
23	Milton	33	Samuelson
41	Tokai	9	Chen
37	Silverberg	43	Shcharanova
5	Benson	24	Manley
7	Brannigan	34	Shappert
30	Quinton	35	Shapton

Note the time taken to complete this Section.

You may now like to take a further short rest before completing the last Section of the test in which your task will be to place items in one of four categories: Animal, Plant, Machine or Human. Identify each by writing the first letter of the appropriate category in front of the noun. When you are ready to begin, start timing yourself and turn the page . . .

____ boy	____ generator
____ grouse	____ dolphin
____ lawnmower	____ hedge
____ grass	____ mole
____ fern	____ servant
____ engineer	____ cement mixer
____ gardener	____ golfer
____ giraffe	____ mushroom
____ automobile	____ drill
____ typewriter	____ landlady
____ daisy	____ scorpion
____ wife	____ pump
____ refrigerator	____ king
____ repairman	____ lotus
____ diver	____ tape recorder
____ moss	____ aunt
____ pigeon	____ ant
____ antelope	____ submarine
____ lathe	____ briar
____ hairdryer	____ truck
____ oak	____ Scot
____ Swede	____ reed

Stop. Record your time for this task.

HOW TO MARK THE TEST

SCORING FOR ERRORS

Section One

Use the scoring key below to check your answers in this Section. Make a note of the total number of errors made.

(1) D	(7) D	(13) D	(19) D	(25) S
(2) D	(8) S	(14) S	(20) S	(26) D
(3) S	(9) D	(15) D	(21) S	(27) S
(4) D	(10) S	(16) D	(22) S	(28) D
(5) D	(11) S	(17) S	(23) D	(29) D
(6) S	(12) D	(18) D	(24) D	(30) D

Section Two

The two scoring keys below indicate with a diagonal line each symbol you should have crossed out. Award yourself an error score of **1 point** for every symbol which you *failed* to delete or for any crossed out by mistake.

Part One

HU8H6SS3B89L3X7CW3GJS6R431HL8Y7BXRG4G2AEW947UXFP9V
QLS5WA6Z89JLDY37Y6GHUD8BV1J6LEB8D6YKI2DT5KFY76LXZ4
PL9KMN7FYEW36VZX2JI1L8RQW721IJGBU9KB3S5CRWQZ7JQ31GY
WHLPB9MN1IF2L93KX3Z7USILT1U5XP6NW89XPQXV7NIZLIT8SW
XPAH4AY9PF3WBNKSR6TILD5J7T1LKCSKEWB6SAL37KA1W7MZXQ
PMNZD46GS8RTWX2J1LFE8CZSA7KDR5PS63MJDTIQESAIIS2BC6

Part Two

MNZØHWØFØVXZWLØNØØWØTPHØYFNØZXRØPØLKYØDØKJSØUCØGQU
KTDXØØTXØPIØBFØGCØUQØUCQØUØØUCSØUØNJFXEDJØWQØCUQGØ
ØCGSAØYTUØMØXJDRHSQUCGSAWBJØPØØGYJØGSØGPØRESZXØCUQ
UCGQUØGCQUGVUNCQØCFSXRNKJHGQØUIFDSCØZØMØBØHGSZRQCU
JYDXEWASDØYHJØØHVFDXCUQØGFRØMØNKØZSDFGDSAZERTWØPLØP
CØREQUØTARØPEDØSERUTENQTSUØPØPERØTEGØCUØTRUCKUGSQPØ
ZSØUØGØGØGUCQUQUCØQCHTDAKØFDTRDØPHØHØØØHVDSAZETTFDØGØ

Section Three

The key below gives the *correct* numbering scheme with ticks indicating items that were incorrectly numbered on the test. Give yourself **1 point** for each misnumbering that you failed to spot.

√	26	McInnes	√	41	Smythe
	1	Alphonse		21	Jarulska
√	40	Smith		14	Haalmi
√	7	Brennan		19	Inigo
√	44	Zelinski	√	3	Anderton
√	13	Gomez	√	2	Anderson
	32	Roebuck	√	25	Matsuhashi
	8	Bunday	√	29	Perigio
√	39	Silverman	√	16	Hansen
	4	Becker	√	12	Gomes
√	33	Roehampton		20	Jacobi
√	23	Koumi	√	22	Kellerman
√	42	Takahashi		28	Paolo
	15	Hampton		10	Chu
√	17	Hanssen		11	Ginsberg
	18	Hodges	√	30	Quigly
√	27	Milton	√	34	Samuelson
√	43	Tokai		9	Chen
√	38	Silverberg	√	37	Shcharanova
	5	Benson		24	Manley
√	6	Brannigan	√	35	Shappert
√	31	Quinton	√	36	Shapton

Section Four

Use the score key below as for Section Three above. You should give yourself **1 point** for each item incorrectly lettered.

H	boy	M	automobile	A	pigeon
A	grouse	M	typewriter	A	antelope
M	lawnmower	P	daisy	M	lathe
P	grass	H	wife	M	hairdryer
P	fern	M	refrigerator	P	oak
H	engineer	H	repairman	H	Swede
H	gardener	H	diver	M	generator
A	giraffe	P	moss	A	dolphin

P hedge	H landlady	A ant
A mole	A scorpion	M submarine
H servant	M pump	P briar
M cement mixer	H king	M truck
H golfer	P lotus	H Scot
P mushroom	M tape recorder	P reed
M drill	H aunt	

Total up your points on all four Sections to obtain the total error score.

SCORING FOR SPEED

All you have to do to obtain this score is simply to total the time taken to complete each of the four Sections.

My Total Error Score =
   My Total Speed =

Where your results place you   The charts below show you where your scores on this test place you in comparison with others who have taken this test.

Errors	**20 or more**	**9–19**	**8 or less**
Your standing	below average	about average	above average

For example, an error score of 7 places you in the company of above average scorers.

Speed	**more than 15 mins.**	**12–15 mins.**	**less than 12 mins.**
Your standing	below average	about average	above average

WHAT THIS TEST TELLS YOU ABOUT YOURSELF

Although reading ability plays a small part in a person's overall performance on this test, the most important mental factor it assesses is what psychologists call 'perceptual processing'.

In simple terms, this means the *speed and accuracy* with which your mind is able to absorb visual information, process it and then come up with the required response. Tests of this factor are often included in assessments used to determine so-called 'clerical aptitude'. But your perceptual processing scores say far more about abilities and personality than merely a suitability for doing paperwork!

According to the balance between speed and accuracy revealed by the test, people can be divided into two broad categories. In general, which category you belong to is determined more by temperament and outlook than by any single intellectual attribute you possess. In addition to identifying important aspects of your aptitude for certain types of work, therefore, this test can provide valuable insights into your overall character and attitudes.

What your scores reveal

Tests completed in less than 12 minutes. Number of errors less than 9. — Your scores identify you as a **Fast-Accurate Thinker**. The shorter the time taken to complete the test and the lower your error score, the more strongly this is indicated. For a full explanation of what this means in terms of work potential and leisure activities, see the detailed notes below.

Tests completed in more than 15 minutes. Number of errors less than 9. — This result identifies you as a **Slow-Accurate Thinker**. The longer the time taken to complete the test and the lower your error score, the more strongly this trait is suggested. For a full explanation of what this means in terms of work potential and leisure activities, see the detailed notes below.

The Fast-Accurate Thinker

You have an ability to combine speed with accuracy when dealing with almost any kind of detailed information. The above-average level of concentration you bring to such tasks indicates that you will be more efficient than most when carrying out tasks that are intricate yet repetitive.

A score which places you in this category also suggests that you have a higher-than-usual level of activity and will be strongly motivated to keep yourself busy, moving and thinking quickly, filling both work and leisure time with considerable variety and change. You probably find it difficult to tolerate inefficiency or poor workmanship on the part of others and become impatient if you are delayed while going about your daily business. This desire to be constantly on the go is likely to make it hard for you fully to relax, since periods of relative inactivity (such as holidays) make you feel unsettled and anxious to be doing something more demanding.

In your work

You should choose a job which enables you to give expression to your talent for handling complex information quickly yet exactly. There is a wide variety of occupations that offer such a challenge, ranging from supervisory duties in an office to working in the hectic atmosphere of a TV studio, a newspaper office or an air traffic control tower.

Most jobs demand a variety of mental attributes and you cannot determine your suitability or otherwise for a particular career solely on the basis of *one* test result. Where handling information with speed and thoroughness is an important consideration, however, your mental superiority in this direction should contribute greatly to a successful performance.

For anybody attracted by the routine of an office, there are numerous activities well suited to the mind of the Fast-Accurate Thinker. You might, for instance, derive satisfaction from some form of clerical work involving filing, sorting, classifying and – especially – checking other people's written work for errors.

The test was constructed so as to include information that was either meaningless (such as strings of letters), or could only be fully understood by a specialist (mathematical formulae, chemical names and so forth). Your ability to deal with this kind of diverse and incomprehensible material speedily and with a minimum amount of errors shows that dealing with unfamiliar facts and figures should present few problems. This is important, since office administrators must frequently check documents containing technical expressions or foreign phrases unknown to them.

You would also be good at keeping accounts, making up wages, preparing and sorting files and indexes. In fact, Fast-Accurate Thinkers generally excel at any tasks which require routine operations to be performed quickly but with constant care.

If you are interested in technology, your talents should enable you to make an efficient punch-card or computer operator. In the first job you would have little difficulty in meeting the challenge of swiftly and accurately transferring written information and data to punched cards or tapes. As a computer operator you would be equally well qualified by your mental make-up to ensure that each processing job ran smoothly, so that costly computer time is never wasted.

Technology of a high order is also involved in working as an air traffic controller or as a radar operator with either the civilian or military authorities. In both these, somewhat similar, occupations, an essential intellectual qualification is the capacity to concentrate for extended periods and to deal continuously with routine activities without becoming careless. With aircraft landing every few seconds during peak times at international airports, and the radar screens crowded with converging white blobs, the traffic controller's ability for fast-accurate thinking can, literally, spell the difference between life and death for hundreds of people.

The same talent should allow you to prove highly effective in the financial world, especially as a member of a firm of stock-brokers or currency dealers. The need to keep constantly up to date with moment-by-moment changes that occur during every working day demands a high level of ability in processing written information with the greatest possible speed and accuracy.

Your desire for variety and change, plus your high level of activity, might make you shy away from jobs involving too much routine, even though you have the ability to cope well in such situations. If this is the case you may prefer to apply the same skills to journalism, advertising, publishing, television or radio.

In all these jobs there is usually considerable pressure to produce accurate work within a limited amount of time and to meet the challenge of inflexible deadlines. The unpredictable nature of such occupations often exerts a strong appeal for people who are Fast-Accurate Thinkers, since it allows them to focus their above-average energies on tasks that also make heavy demands on their other mental skills.

In your leisure time

You should consider sports requiring rapid decision making and accurate responses, for example tennis, boxing, judo, karate, fencing and squash, where you must react quickly and precisely to your opponent's moves. Provided you are in sound physical health, your skill in pursuits of this type will probably be greater than that of other players of the same age.

The Slow-Accurate Thinker

Your test scores indicate that, when handling detailed information, you prefer to proceed slowly but surely in order to make certain nothing of importance is overlooked. You probably feel compelled to check each detail several times, you dislike being put under too much pressure and will refuse to be rushed when working on an intricate task. You are more patient than most and so excel in work and leisure activities that demand considerable persistence.

In your work
Your methodical approach to complex tasks makes you ideally suited to any activity which places a premium on care, patience and persistence while allowing you to work at your own pace.

If you are interested in books, for example, then librarianship could offer the kind of environment which favours your somewhat unhurried but thorough attitude towards work. Your eye for detail will enable you to do especially well at such tasks as cataloguing, filing, classifying or research, provided that none of these has to be completed against an urgent deadline.

If you favour an outdoor life and a physically more demanding career, then many jobs in the construction industry could suit your particular mental ability: for instance, bricklaying, plastering, woodworking, plumbing and glazing. Horticulture too offers many opportunities for people who are methodical enough to take care of essential details when rearing delicate plants, yet patient enough not to mind waiting weeks or months before seeing the results of their labours.

A Slow-Accurate Thinker who is fond of do-it-yourself or practical hobbies might also consider decorating, since the precision and patience required when painting, papering, resurfacing floors and so on would provide ample job-satisfaction. Other careers especially suitable to anybody with this type of mind are bookbinding, boatbuilding, furniture making, working as a silver-smith, weaving, embroidery, metalworking and plastics work.

In the professions, many aspects of legal work, especially those involving civil litigation or the preparation of lengthy and detailed briefs could prove attractive. In science or medicine your talents could most enjoyably be challenged in research or specializations which allow time for thought, where success depends on meticulous planning and careful application.

As we made clear in our Introduction, most occupations require a variety of intellectual attributes and it would be foolish to believe you can determine your suitability or otherwise for a particular career on the basis of only *one* assessment result. However, it is fairly certain that your aptitude for being persistent and methodical when handling complex information will serve you best in tasks where care and diligence, rather than speed of response, are the keys to success.

In your leisure time

You are likely to do best at sports which require concentration and an eye for detail, without placing players under too much pressure to react quickly. Your mental make-up is especially suited to pursuits such as golf, snooker, billiards, croquet, bowling, archery, fishing and target shooting. Similarly, the kind of hobby to give you most satisfaction will probably be one which demands patience and care in order to accomplish it successfully. Such activities include restoring antiques, model making, painting, photography, stamp collecting, print making, weaving, gardening, knitting, calligraphy, computer programming, crosswords or any form of puzzles, chess and complicated board games, electronics and bird watching.

To sum up

If you worked fast and made few errors, you have the kind of mind which handles detailed information quickly and accurately. This suggests you can best employ your brain on tasks which demand a quick response-time and offer rapid results. You should avoid occupations, or leisure-time activities, that depend on a methodical attention to fine detail for their ultimate success.

If you worked slowly and made few errors, the keynote of your mental approach to complex information is one of persistence combined with care. You will find the best match for your mind in jobs needing constant vigilance within a fairly well-structured routine. In your leisure-time activities, sports or pursuits which require the same intellectual attributes will prove most satisfying. Avoid careers where you have to work fast under the kind of pressure that makes it impossible to do anything as perfectly as you would like.

ASSESSMENT TWO

HOW TO TAKE THIS TEST

In this test you are going to be given words in a foreign language, together with their English equivalents, and sentences illustrating the way in which they are used.

Read the words and the sample sentences carefully and then translate the numbered phrases which follow. In some instances you will be required to translate from English into the foreign language, at other times the task will be to rewrite the foreign-language sentence in English.

Start by going through the practice example below so that you are familiar with the test procedure.

Vocabulary

aknum = man
napra = child
murti = woman
li = and
tov = has
setiv = knows
hamnav = accompanies
os = the
ne = a

Sample sentence

Ne napra hamnav os murti. = A child accompanies the woman.

PRACTICE QUESTIONS

(1) The woman accompanies a man.
(2) Os murti setiv os aknum li os napra.
(3) The woman has a child.
(4) Os aknum hamnav ne murti.

Work through these sentences, in order to get a feel for the task, before looking at the answers overleaf.

Answers to practice questions

(1) Os murti hamnav ne aknum.
(2) The woman knows the man and the child.
(3) Os murti tov ne napra.
(4) The man accompanies a woman.

Before starting the test, here are some general hints which will help you achieve the best possible score. Avoid spending too long on any one problem since this is a timed test and you will have only a few minutes to work on it. If you get stuck at any point, go on to the next question and return to any sentences you may have failed to translate if time allows at the end. In some of the sentences you will be asked to use a word or a fact that occurred several questions earlier. In others, you may have to translate a sentence for which the precise words have not been given. This is done deliberately in order to assess the extent of certain basic language skills. If you find that the exact words have not been supplied, make use of the vocabulary and constructional rules you are familiar with in order to produce the closest translation possible.

You should allow yourself exactly 30 minutes to complete this test, stopping as soon as the time is up, whether or not you have finished.

Do not turn over this page until you are ready to start. As soon as you do turn the page, start timing the test.

ap nameh = the brother
ar esnak = the cat
esnak-go = my cat
opu = to see
Esnak nameha-go opat. = A cat sees my brother.

(1) My cat sees.
(2) Nameh-go esnaka opat.
(3) The brother sees my cat.

to swim = poro
to want = nlepu
you = bak
Do you want to swim? = Nlepasag bak poro soh?

(4) Do you swim?
(5) Nlepasag bak nameh-go poro soh?
(6) Does my brother want to see my cat?

ap mrutam = the father
mrutam-bako = your father
agratu = to be able to
Dos agratat poro. = He is able to swim.

(7) Can your brother swim?
(8) Nlepat mrutam-go esnaka-bako opu soh?
(9) Can he see my brother?

ap banam = the boy
ar sevarpulet = the bicycle
apul namehul = the brothers
they = sul
matugo = to buy

(10) Sul agratakag ara sevarpuleta matugo.
(11) Do the boys want to see my brother?
(12) Ap banam u nameh-sed nlepakag arula sevarpuletula matugo.
(13) Did you see the boys?

the automobile = ar fegaramet
to drive = negabu
she = doj
well = nasam

You bought an automobile. = Bak fegarameta matugeg.

(14) Ap banam ara sevarpuleta matugeg.
(15) Are you a good driver?
(16) They drive the automobiles.

the house = ar kafnat
to go = mui
to stay = samui

She wanted to stay in her house. = Doj nleseg nar kafnati-sej samui.

(17) Dos u doj mui dar kafnatok nlesakag.
(18) He goes to my house in his car.

aduli = to give
geftaru = to tell
soteh = here
ar kupardet = the mother
ap famatar = the book

Gat kupardetud-go esnaka adulesk. = I gave my mother a cat.

(19) His father gives the boy a book.
(20) She told his father and his mother to stay in the house.
(21) Geftaril nameh-bako ara fegarameta dar kafnati-go negabu.
(22) Soteh bat ap famatar kupardet-sed baku adulesk.
(23) Did your father want to be able to give you a book?

HOW TO MARK THE TEST

Answers

(1) Esnak-go opat.
(2) My brother sees a cat.
(3) Ap nameh esnaka-go opat.
(4) Porasag bak soh?
(5) Do you want my brother to swim?
(6) Nlepat nameh-go esnaka-go opu soh?
(7) Agratat nameh-bako poro soh?
(8) Does my father want to see your cat?
(9) Agratat dos nameha-go opu soh?
(10) They are able to buy the bicycle.
(11) Nlepakag apul banamul nameha-go opu soh?
(12) The boy and his brother want to buy the bicycles.
(13) Opasag bak apula banamula soh?
(14) The boy bought the bicycle.
(15) Negabasag bak nasam soh?
(16) Sul arula fegarametula negabakag.
(17) He and she want to go to the house.
(18) Dos dar kafnatok-go nar fegarameti mued.
(19) Mrutam-sed apud banamud famatara aduled.
(20) Doj mrutamud-sed u kupardetud-sed nar kafnati samui geftaresk.
(21) Tell your brother to drive the automobile to my house.
(22) Here is the book his mother gave you.
(23) Nlepeg mrutam-bako aduli baku famatara agratu soh? or Nlepeg mrutam-bako baku famatara agratu aduli soh?

Compare your answers with those just given. Award yourself **1 point** for each word which is both correct *and* properly located in the sentence. Give yourself a **half-point** for each word which is correct and properly located, but misspelled (this would include any '-s' you may have left out).

Suppose, for instance, you have given the following translation for Question 18:

Das mued dar kafnatok go nar fegaramet.
↑   ↑   ↑   ↑

The correct translation should be:

Dos dar kafnatok-go nar fegarameti mued.

In the incorrect translation above, arrows are used to point out the four mistakes that were made. 'Das' has been incorrectly spelled, 'mued' is misplaced in the sentence, the hyphen in front of '-go' is missing and the ending '-i' needed by 'fegaramet' has been left out. When marking this sentence you would get 1 point for 'dar', 1 for 'kafnatok' and 1 for 'nar' – all of which have been correctly translated, properly placed in the sentence and correctly spelled. In addition, you would receive a half-point for 'go' which is correctly translated and placed, but misspelled due to the omission of the hyphen. Finally you would receive a further half-point for 'Das' which is also correct in every way except in its spelling. No points can be given for 'mued' or 'fegaramet' which are incorrectly placed in the sentence. This means that the answer given above would score a total of 4 points (3 full points and 2 half-points).

Study this example and then go through each of your own translations in this manner, writing down the total points for every sentence. Add up these totals to obtain your final test score.

My total score =

Where your results place you   The chart below indicates how your score on this test compares to the rest of the people taking this test.

Score	**less than 48**	**48–69**	**70 or more**
Your standing	below average	about average	above average

WHAT THIS TEST TELLS YOU ABOUT YOURSELF

As you may have guessed, the language used in this test is not spoken anywhere on earth. It was created for assessment purposes in order to bring together characteristics found in many genuine languages. This gives the test what psychologists describe as *content validity*, or the ability to make a systematic and exhaustive assessment of a particular area of mental functioning.

The test has been designed to measure a number of different factors that together make up an aptitude for languages. You will have noticed that the questions often required you to recall vocabulary words or language rules that had been used several sentences earlier. This was done deliberately in order to assess *working memory*, one of the most important mental skills you need to make use of when acquiring a new language. As the name suggests, this refers to the store in which relevant information is held while some task is being carried out. For instance, after looking up a telephone number, you might need to hold it in your working memory, rather than noting it down, while dialling.

When working through a foreign-language lesson, this process of recalling recently acquired knowledge plays an important role in fixing that information in long-term storage so that it can be recalled easily. Clearly then, the more efficient your working memory, the more rapidly essential words and rules of structure will be transferred to permanent storage and the quicker you will become proficient in their use. A great deal of language learning also arises when you hold conversations with native-born speakers. Here again, you are exposed to a wealth of new information, such as unfamiliar words and phrases, slang expressions, and ways of constructing or stressing certain sentences. This information is likely to be presented briefly and may occur only once or twice during the exchange. The greater the proportion of this important material that you can retain for subsequent transfer into long-term storage, the faster you will become fluent in that language.

A second component of language aptitude, which this test measured, is an ability to generalize aspects of grammar and syntax from one sentence to another. This is important, because all languages have a core structure on which conversation is based. The more effectively a learner is able to fit specific examples on to this structure, the more easily that language will be mastered.

When using another language, you will inevitably find that there are occasions when you need to say or write something without having yet learned the precise words to express your meaning. At times like this the proficient linguist exercises great ingenuity in adapting vocabulary and phrases that he or she knows to meet the demands of the unfamiliar situation. Examples of this problem were contained in the test, when certain questions required you to adapt previously used words in order to express the correct meaning.

If you scored above average on this test, you can be confident of possessing the ability to learn foreign languages well and with relative ease. *Which* ones are best suited to your skills? Clearly your choice here will, to some extent at least, be determined by whatever interest you may have in the culture, literature and people of a particular country, or perhaps by the requirements of a particular occupation.

Since each language has its own special characteristics and unique aspects of grammar, syntax and vocabulary, however, it is often useful to know which, of the more than 2,000 spoken languages identified by linguistic experts, is most likely to suit your mental abilities.

Now that your general aptitude for language learning has been established, we will consider how you can use the test to decide which language or languages might be acquired most easily and enjoyably. The list below contains the languages which, our research has shown, are most commonly studied at night school and by students attending courses of further education. They are listed in *approximate* order of difficulty for native speakers of English starting with the least difficult. This is only a general guide, however, and ought not to deter you from studying a language further down the list.

Romance Languages	*Slavic Languages*
French	Czech
Italian	Serbo-Croatian
Portuguese	Polish
Spanish	Bulgarian
	Russian
Teutonic Languages	
Dutch	*Oriental Languages*
German	Japanese
Norwegian	Chinese
Swedish	
Danish	*Ural-Altaic Languages*
	Hungarian
Indo-European Languages	Finnish
Modern Greek	
Latin	*Gulf-State Languages*
	Arabic
	Farsi

To determine which of these languages you are most likely to master with the least amount of difficulty, reflect back on what was going on in your mind as you took the test.

You will remember that nouns in the specially created language around which the questions were based took various endings, depending on how they were used in the sentence. For example, in Question (2) 'Nameh-go esnaka opat', the word for cat, esnak, was given the ending '-a' because it was the object of the sentence. This is a characteristic not met with in English and one which often causes problems for native English speakers in languages where it is found. In the test, these endings, called *declensions*, appeared in every sentence except Questions 1, 4, 5, 7, 15 and 22. If the misuse of declensions produced an error in more than a *quarter* of the words in which they were used, you might feel more comfortable learning a language which does not employ such a device. The Romance languages, for instance, contain no declensions, but all the Slavic languages make use of them; in Russian there are six. This means that when translating such phrases as 'to the girl', 'with the girl', 'for the girl' and 'of the girl' into Russian, a different ending for 'girl' will be needed each time. German utilizes declensions to a lesser extent, as does modern Greek. The record-holders, however, are Hungarian and Finnish, the former having more than a dozen.

Another interesting feature of certain languages, and one which was also reflected in the test, is the use of what are called *linguistic particles*, words which shade the meaning of a sentence in which they are used. The closest we come to the use of linguistic particles in English would be in employing a word like 'just' in a sentence such as, 'Just turn down the TV.' Here, 'just' does not have any individual meaning but serves to add emphasis to the command. German makes far greater use of such emphatic words than English. For example the sentence, 'It is just around the corner!' may be translated into German as, 'It is yes finally certainly just even around the corner!'

The German emphatic *Fullwörter* or 'fill words' will not cause the learner much trouble, but there are more subtle variations of the linguistic particle that may pose problems at first. In the test, the use of the word 'soh' as an *interrogative particle* (or kind of question mark) exemplifies a feature found in many Oriental languages, including Japanese and all the Chinese dialects. Its use in these languages is dictated by the fact that the native speakers do not alter voice pitch to express a question. To convey the fact that the spoken phrase, 'That is your best offer?' is a question rather than a statement, we need only raise the pitch of the final word. When speaking Chinese or Japanese, this distinction has to be communicated by the use of special words. The Japanese also make use of numerous linguistic particles that subtly influence meaning in a variety of ways, while the Chinese rely on particles to clarify the meaning of particular words and form an important part of that language's vocabulary. If you encountered problems with the use of 'soh' in the test and made a number of errors when employing the particle, you should consider whether this might impede your learning of an Oriental language.

You will also have noticed that the word-order of the test language did not correspond exactly to that of English, especially in the placement of verbs which always came at the end. Look back through your answers and see whether this unfamiliar sentence-structure caused any problems for you. If it was responsible for producing two or more errors, then it is important to pay special attention to word-order in any language you wish to study. In most languages, noticeable differences will be encountered from the earliest days of study: in German and Japanese, for instance, where the verb comes at the end of the sentence. In Spanish, the adjective usually follows the noun and this also happens quite frequently in French.

Other significant sources of error that the test might have revealed are difficulties in coping with the lack of the indefinite article 'a' in the made-up language. This is not uncommon in many genuine foreign languages, most notably Russian and Polish. Trouble could also have arisen due to the attachment of possessive pronouns (my, his, etc.) to the ends of the nouns they modified: for example, 'Nameh-go' which translated as 'my brother', with the suffix '-go' indicating 'my'. Such a form of construction is also fairly common, occurring, for example, in modern Greek and Arabic.

A final quality of the test language, and one which is shared to some extent with almost *any* language you decide to learn, is the fact that it 'sounds strange'. Many of our subjects have commented on how weird the test language seemed at first, and this fact is of more than passing importance. When learning a foreign vocabulary, the task becomes far less arduous if the words can be pronounced fairly easily. This is because silently repeating words as you read them (subvocalization, as it is called), plays an important part in aiding recall. The words in the test were deliberately created to produce unusual sounds so as to make the work of memorizing them just that little bit harder: for instance, the letter combination 'mr' in 'mrutam' does not occur at the start of any English word.

If subvocalizing the test language proved especially difficult because of its phonetic idiosyncrasies, then you might have problems in acquiring languages, such as those in the Slavic group, that sound strange to English ears. For example, there is a Czech sound which is written 'ř'; this is pronounced by making a 'zh' sound (like the 'z' in azure) while *simultaneously* trilling an 'r' as in the Scots dialect. This sound occurs in the name of the composer, Dvořák, and is rarely pronounced correctly by the native English speaker.

Because French, Spanish, Italian, Finnish or modern Greek are easier to pronounce than other European languages, their vocabulary often comes more easily to native English speakers.

It is important to realize that these comments are only intended as a general guide to the kind of difficulties people may face when starting to speak a foreign language. If your errors on the assessment suggest that you might find special problems with a particular language, you would be well advised to consult an experienced teacher, or an educated native speaker, to discover just how much of a stumbling block these problems are likely to prove.

To sum up

If you scored above average on the test as a whole, it strongly suggests that you would be able to learn any language far more readily than most people. Use this knowledge, together with any specific sources of error, to guide you towards those languages which you could master most easily and quickly.

ASSESSMENT THREE

HOW TO TAKE THIS TEST

You will be presented with a series of statements that you are to accept as being true. After each, there will be a list of conclusions, derived from information given in the statement, which *may or may not be correct*. Your task is to consider each one in turn and make a judgment about it. You may decide that a particular conclusion is True (T) or that it is Probably True (PT). On the other hand you might feel that there was Insufficient Information (II) on which to base any judgment, or that the conclusion is Probably False (PF) or entirely False (F). Your decision is then indicated by simply circling the appropriate letters, as set out in the example below.

STATEMENT

Sales of men's clothing at Natty's Department Store have fallen off drastically in the last ten months and the management is faced with two possible courses of action. In order to increase sales they can either lower the prices, or spend more on advertising in the local press and on TV. After several meetings and much discussion it is agreed to increase the advertising budget.

Conclusions

(1) The management are worried about the profitability
of the menswear department. T (PT) II PF F

(2) The sales of men's clothing in the store increased. T PT II PF (F)

(3) The management decided on increased advertising
as the most promising measure to improve sales. (T) PT II PF F

(4) Their advertising programme led to an increase in
business in the menswear department. T PT (II) PF F

(5) Almost all the sales decrease occurred in the first
month. T PT II (PF) F

Explanation of the answers

(1) We are told that considerable time was spent discussing losses, so it is probably true the decline in sales caused concern. The correct choice to circle is therefore the PT conclusion.

(2) Since we are told in the statement that sales declined in the menswear department, this conclusion is clearly false, and the letter F must be circled.

(3) We are informed that more money was spent on advertising, which makes this conclusion true, and T is circled.

(4) It may well be true that increased advertising raised sales in the menswear department, but there is insufficient information fully to support that conclusion, and II has to be circled.

(5) If most of the decrease in profits occurred in the first month, the chances are that the management, who seem to be concerned about losses, would have held discussions about the problem earlier on. As we are told that no action was taken until ten months had passed, this conclusion is probably false (PF).

Although there is no time limit, and you do not need to record how long it takes to complete this test, we suggest that you tackle all the problems at one sitting, since this will ensure concentration on the task. Once again we would caution you against marking the book. It is quite sufficient just to note your responses on a separate sheet of paper, if you do not want to photocopy the material.

When you are ready, turn the page and start by reading Statement One.

STATEMENT ONE

A teacher, whose class consists of 35 nine- and ten-year-old children, wishes to raise the standard of arithmetic performance among her pupils. In order to do this, she decides to compare traditional classroom instruction with an alternative method of teaching. The new technique consists of having children solve problems, which have been presented on the screen of a microcomputer, by typing in their answers. The computer informs the child if each solution is correct.

The teacher divides her class into two groups, carefully matched for arithmetic ability on the basis of an educational test. One group continues to receive traditional classroom teaching, while the other goes to a different room to be taught by the computer. After three months, the teacher again tests the arithmetic performance of each group; she finds that those who learned from the microcomputer score 50% better than their companions.

Conclusions

(1) The computer method for learning arithmetic is
    more effective than classroom teaching for children
    in the teacher's class.   T PT II PF F

(2) Children aged nine to ten who are taught arithmetic
    by the computer will learn more than those taught in
    the traditional way.   T PT II PF F

(3) Any other teacher who tries this experiment is
    unlikely to get similar results.   T PT II PF F

(4) The teacher who carried out the experiment will
    adopt the computer method to teach her pupils
    arithmetic.   T PT II PF F

STATEMENT TWO

A biologist is studying a colony of tiny fish which are kept in a tank in the laboratory. These fish feed only on underwater plants. The fish reproduce quite abundantly. The biologist takes a population count once a month; she observes that at each count the fish population has doubled.

Conclusions

(1) The fish population grew more rapidly in the second
month than in the first.   T PT II PF F
(2) In the biologist's tank the population growth will
eventually be curtailed.   T PT II PF F
(3) In their natural habitat, the fish population would be
limited by predators.   T PT II PF F
(4) In the event of a food shortage, the fish will devour
their young.   T PT II PF F

STATEMENT THREE

In a country where the economy is heavily dependent on agriculture, fruit farmers' annual yields are adversely affected each year by two problems: the first is a particular species of fly which destroys a certain proportion of the ripe fruit; the second is a disease which lessens the trees' ability to make use of nourishment, thus limiting their yield. A firm of specialists is called in to carry out a five-year study of the situation. After carefully measuring the fly population and the rate of disease during this period, their scientists make the following observation: the greater the rate of disease, the larger the number of flies that will attack the fruit in any given year. The farmers are assured that this finding is reliable and can be expected to hold true where future fruit-crops are concerned.

Conclusions

(1) There is a relationship between the amount of
diseased trees and the number of flies present.   T PT II PF F
(2) The diseased trees attract flies.   T PT II PF F
(3) Extermination of the flies should prevent the disease. T PT II PF F
(4) The fruit farming industry in the affected area will
not suffer very much if a solution to the problem of
the flies and the disease is not found.   T PT II PF F

STATEMENT FOUR

Doctors in a group practice extracted from their files the names and addresses of every woman who had given birth during the previous three months. A questionnaire was mailed out to the new mothers, asking whether they would like to have received counselling during their pregnancy. Of the women questioned, 30% completed the forms and returned them. Of those responding, 75% stated they would have liked pre-natal counselling.

Conclusions

(1) The doctors believed that pre-natal counselling could prove beneficial to expectant mothers.   T PT II PF F

(2) The majority of expectant mothers in the community would like to have pre-natal counselling.   T PT II PF F

(3) Women over thirty-five were excluded from the study.   T PT II PF F

STATEMENT FIVE

You have just qualified as an accountant and intend to apply for a job with a firm in the country of Sans Serif. You learn from the Serifian Embassy that half the accountants in their country earn less than 10,000 Serifian dollars in their first year of employment, while the other half earn in excess of this sum. Salaries for newly qualified accountants range from 5,000 to 15,000 Serifian dollars during their first twelve months at work.

Conclusions

(1) The average salary earned by Serifian accountants in their first year of employment is 10,000 Serifian dollars.   T PT II PF F

(2) The chances are about even that you will earn more than 10,000 Serifian dollars during your first year's employment.   T PT II PF F

(3) It is likely you will earn a salary between 8,000 and 12,000 Serifian dollars.   T PT II PF F

STATEMENT SIX

A monkey is climbing a 30-foot rope which runs over a pulley above the animal and dangles down in front of it. A stone, attached to the other end of the rope, hangs level with the monkey directly in front of its chest. Their weights are identical. The monkey starts to climb the rope.

Conclusions

(1) Chances are . . . the monkey will get tired and stop
climbing before he reaches the top.   T PT II PF F
(2) . . . the stone remains in the same place as the
monkey climbs.   T PT II PF F
(3) . . . the stone goes up as the monkey climbs.   T PT II PF F
(4) . . . the stone goes down as the monkey climbs.   T PT II PF F

STATEMENT SEVEN

In the suburb of Green Lewes, three times as many traffic accidents occur in
the weekday rush-hour traffic as during the same times at weekends.

Conclusions

(1) This is because it is more dangerous to drive during
the weekday rush-hour period than during the same
hours at weekends.   T PT II PF F
(2) It is more dangerous to drive in Green Lewes during
weekday rush-hours than at weekends during the
same hours.   T PT II PF F

STATEMENT EIGHT

In a recent survey of shopping habits, an interviewer recorded the following
exchange between herself and a shopper:
QUESTION: 'What would you say is the average amount of time you spent on
weekly shopping during the past year?'
ANSWER: 'I estimate that I spent an average of four hours and thirty minutes
per week on shopping in that period.'

Conclusion

The shopper spent an average of four hours and thirty
minutes on weekly shopping during the last year.   T PT II PF F

STATEMENT NINE

Intensive studies by a team of highly paid government zoologists have revealed the following astounding differences between the milk of the Maltese Mountain Mole and that of the Vancouver Variegated Vole. After vast expenditure of taxpayers' money, the researchers discovered that milk from the Mountain Mole curdles far more quickly at room temperature than does the milk of the Variegated Vole. There is, however, no appreciable difference between the milk curdling rates of the two animals when their milk contains similar amounts of the trace chemical, drekamine. The average amount of drekamine is substantially higher in the Vole's milk.

Conclusions

(1) One way to prevent these two animals' unrefrigerated
    milk from curdling is to add drekamine.   T PT II PF F

(2) Animals' milk containing a large amount of
    drekamine is less likely to curdle than that which
    contains a small amount.   T PT II PF F

(3) Mole's milk containing high amounts of drekamine
    will take longer to curdle than low drekamine milk
    from the same animal, if both samples are stored at
    room temperatures.   T PT II PF F

(4) A vial of milk from either a Mole or a Vole was placed
    on the Minister's coffee table. It curdled in two
    minutes (the average curdling time for milk is
    twenty-four hours) and thus must have come from a
    Mole.   T PT II PF F

(5) If milk comes from a Mole, whether it has a high
    drekamine content or a low drekamine content
    makes no differences to its chances of curdling.   T PT II PF F

The final part of this test takes a slightly different form. We want you to read the script of a television commercial broadcast by the Enam-Off Toothpaste Company and, after first deciding on the validity of their claims, to list as many reasons you can think of in support of your conclusions.

STATEMENT TEN

'Good news for all parents from Enam-Off Toothpaste Limited, the company that really cares for your teeth! To prove scientifically that new, enriched Enam-Off toothpaste – with the magic ingredient, 666 – not only cleans your teeth whiter and brighter but also stops cavities dead in their tracks, we carried out a carefully controlled dental study. We asked a group of school-children, at the worst age for cavities, to brush daily with Enam-Off. Then we compared their dental records with a large group of children who used several other well-known brands regularly. When the results were analysed, it was found that Enam-Off's three-way protection shone through bright and clear. The Enam-Off youngsters had NO NEW CAVITIES during the entire period!'

Conclusion

If you brush your teeth with Enam-Off, you are less
likely to develop cavities than if you used another brand. T PT II PF F

HOW TO MARK THE TEST

Use the key below to check your answers, placing a tick by each one which is incorrect. Then look through our list of reasons why the Enam-Off conclusions are based on insufficient information. These are not necessarily exhaustive, and you may have spotted some flaws in their research which we have missed. If so, and you feel your criticisms are as justified as those listed, then award yourself **1 point** for each of them. Every criticism is worth 1 point and if you came up with more than 7 of those listed in the answer key below then award yourself an additional 8 points.

Answers to test items

Statement One
(1) T (2) II (3) PF (4) PT

Statement Six
(1) PF (2) F (3) T (4) F

Statement Two
(1) T (2) T (3) II (4) PF

Statement Seven
(1) II (2) II

Statement Three
(1) T (2) II (3) II (4) PF

Statement Eight
PF

Statement Four
(1) PT (2) II (3) F

Statement Nine
(1) II (2) PT (3) T
(4) PT (5) F

Statement Five
(1) II (2) T (3) II

Statement Ten
II

In Statement Ten, the correct response (that there is insufficient information on which to assess Enam-Off's claim) is justified as follows:

(1) The results from the control group (those children who brushed with other brands of toothpaste) are not given. Perhaps they also reported no cavities.

(2) No information is given about the type of examination carried out to detect cavities, i.e. visual inspection, X-rays, or other techniques.

(3) We are not told whether the inspection was carried out by qualified dental surgeons.

(4) We do not know whether the two groups of children were matched for age and socio-economic background, both factors which could have influenced the outcome.

(5) We do not know what sort of a diet the children in each group enjoyed. If one group ate, say, many more sweet foods, this could have influenced the chances of cavities occurring.

(6) We do not know anything about parental attitudes towards eating sweets between meals or how closely such behaviour was supervised.

(7) We do not know how long it was before the study took place that children in each group had received dental care.

(8) We are not told how many children there were in either the control group or the Enam-Off study group. The smaller the number, the less meaningful the results.

(9) We do not know how many other brands were used by the children in the control group.

(10) We are not told whether any check was made to ensure that the Enam-Off group actually followed their instructions to brush their teeth daily.

(11) We have no information about any other dental hygiene habits employed by the children in the two groups. For instance, did some brush their teeth more than once a day, perhaps after every meal, or use dental floss to clean between the teeth or a plaque dye to check on the thoroughness of their cleaning?

(12) We are not told over what period of time the study was carried out – it would not be at all surprising if no cavities showed up after only a few weeks.

(13) We do not know in which country the trial was carried out – cultural differences might account for the results.

(14) We do not know whether children in the study group were matched with those in the control group according to the initial condition of their teeth.

(15) We do not know how the children were selected for inclusion in each group. If such a choice was made on other than a *random* basis, this could have introduced bias into the study.

(16) We are not told whether any independent verification was made of the Enam-Off Company's findings.

Total your score, and remember to award yourself an 8-point bonus if you found seven or more good reasons for concluding that the Enam-Off company's claims were – at best – not proven.

My total score =

WHAT THIS TEST TELLS YOU ABOUT YOURSELF

The test has been constructed to measure your aptitude for scientific think-ing. This is an ability to make sound judgments about data on the basis of their information content alone. The table below shows where your score places you in this important area of mental activity.

What your scores reveal

0–22   A slightly lower-than-average score which suggests that your reasoning is not subject to the restrictions that making detailed critical judgments demands. This should not be taken to imply that you are a vague, muddle-headed individual. On the contrary, many highly creative people – particularly those with a strong interest in arts subjects – obtain a below-average score on this test. To be successful in many creative areas it is often necessary, initially, to cast aside any, or all, restrictions on evaluative judgment and decision mak-ing. There are many styles of thinking, some highly suitable for a given intellectual activity and others less helpful.

23–33   This is an average score which indicates that, while you have a certain talent for scientific reasoning, you prob-ably have little difficulty in casting aside the restraints of logical thought when it comes to tasks requiring a more intuitive, emotional response. It may be that, in the past, you have had little opportunity to practise the kind of thinking needed to make precise and objective judgments on the basis of statements you have heard or read about. Even if you do not work in the scientific field, and have no interest in doing so, it will pay you to develop this mental ability to a higher level, since being able to detect the weaknesses in other people's argu-ments and conclusions can safeguard you from making many types of mistakes – and even offer protection from the often wildly inaccurate claims of advertisers.

34 or more   Your score is above average and shows that you have a good aptitude for scientific thinking. What it could mean to your way of life, and how you should make the most of the ability, are discussed in greater detail below.

What it means to think scientifically

When dealing with scientific matters, it is important to remain objective and not read extra information into the facts to hand. If this does happen, it may cause you to draw false conclusions and so waste time and energy in an unpromising branch of research.

Another important element in scientific thinking, which was also measured by the test, is the ability to read conclusions from incomplete information, since it quite often happens that theories must be formulated on little factual evidence. Einstein used to liken a scientist to somebody seeing a watch for the first time, and attempting to find out how it worked merely by observing the movement of the hands!

The evaluation of other researchers' experimental work plays a vital role in the life of almost every scientist, which is why the Enam-Off problem was included in the test. It is fairly typical of the type of claim one sometimes comes across in advertisements, in that it omits a large amount of information crucial to any judgment as to the merit, or otherwise, of the research being described.

The important part of any scientific experiment begins long before a researcher starts gathering data. All worthwhile investigations are preceded by a considerable amount of time and effort devoted to going through learned papers on the same subject and objectively evaluating the results and conclusions of these experiments. It is from this foundation of knowledge that the scientist constructs theories and makes predictions. To be successful in such a task, the researcher must have a keen nose for smelling out the weak and strong points of the experimental reports that play such an important role in shaping the thinking and planning of new work. If you were able to list more than half the reasons we gave for mistrusting the Enam-Off claims, you have an aptitude for analysing experimental results. This means you should be good at taking the right decision when considering whether to accept or reject another researcher's conclusions.

The fact that scientific thinking is objective and logical does not mean there is no room for flashes of inspiration or the exercise of great imagination. Indeed, little progress could have been made in science but for those intuitive leaps of understanding which are the keynote of great scientific genius. Because you obtained an above-average score on this test does not therefore mean that you are lacking in originality or the capacity to respond to events in other than an analytical manner. The key difference between yourself and somebody in whom scientific-thinking aptitude is less well developed is that you possess a facility for refining creative visions and translating them into reality.

It is important to understand that although the term 'scientific thinking' describes an aptitude essential for the type of objective reasoning required in experimental work, this does not mean that such intellectual ability is of value only in the world of science. Exactly the same mental skills can usefully be employed in many areas of industry, allowing commercial decisions to be taken more surely and complex business problems solved far more readily.

Where scientific studies are concerned, your high score should allow you to do equally well in any area of study from chemistry and physics to the life sciences of biology, ecology, botany, zoology, physiology and neurology. You may be more interested in the social sciences, psychology, sociology, political science, economics and anthropology, or such earth sciences as geology and meteorology. Perhaps electronics or computer science is of interest, or you could be attracted by such diverse activities as cybernetics (the study of organic and inorganic systems and their interaction with the environment), palaeontology or archaeology.

Away from the laboratory bench, you might find equally stimulating challenges in the office and company boardroom where the objective analysis of highly detailed information may be critical to a company's success. A good example of the need for a scientific approach to the challenges of the commercial world can be found in the work of an insurance underwriter. In order to determine the degree of risk associated with a new policy the company wishes to launch, an underwriter must be able to analyse a large volume of data, some of which may be incomplete or consist of the unsubstantiated notions of others. The material has to be examined critically so as to discover how much of the evidence is valid, which facts are suspect and what conclusions can safely be drawn – exactly the same sort of tasks which confronted you in the test. Finally, far-reaching conclusions must be made regarding the potential profitability of the risk being undertaken. In this, as in many other areas of business activity, the situation presents a picture very similar to that found in much laboratory research.

To sum up

In any area of mental activity where a premium is placed on thorough analysis and ordered, objective reasoning, your above-average aptitude for scientific thinking should allow you to excel.

ASSESSMENT FOUR

HOW TO TAKE THIS TEST

This test is divided into three sections, all of which have to be completed within specific time limits. Read through the instructions below so as to familiarize yourself with what is required in Section One. You will find instructions for the remaining sections at the start of each.

SECTION ONE

In this section you will be given two problems that both involve writing down as many words as possible which share a particular characteristic. For instance, you might be asked to list all the words that end in '-able'. In this case, your answer could include *available, sable, stable, table* . . . and so on. Continue to do this until your time is up and then stop immediately.

PART ONE

(to be completed in 60 seconds)

Get your watch ready and start timing yourself as soon as you turn the page. Remember to **stop writing at the end of one minute**.

You are to write down as many words as possible which begin with (start timing yourself now and turn the page) . . .

. . . the letters '**GU**'. Start writing *now*.

With Part One completed, take a rest of one minute and then get ready for Part Two.

PART TWO

(to be completed in 2 minutes)

This time we want you to write down as many words as possible which begin with (start timing yourself now and turn the page) . . .

. . . an '**A**', and end with '**E**'. Start writing *now*.

This completes Section One. Now allow yourself a break of about 10 minutes before starting on Section Two.

SECTION TWO

In this section you will be given the name of a common object and asked to write down as many different uses as possible to which it might be put. For example, if asked to list possible uses for a 'brick' you might note down such ideas as – 'building a house', 'heat up and use to warm a bed', 'as a bookend', etc.

This part has to be completed in **7 minutes**.

The object for which you are to list as many different, and varied, uses as possible is (start timing yourself now and turn the page) . . .

. . . A FLOWER POT. Start writing *now*.

That completes Section Two. Give yourself a ten-minute break before moving on to Section Three.

SECTION THREE

In this final part of the test, write down all the consequences you believe would arise if a particular event occurred. If for example that event was 'an automobile accident', you might list such outcomes as: 'the drivers going to court'; 'the cars involved being repaired'; 'road widened to prevent further accidents . . .', etc.

This Section must be completed in **15 minutes**.

You are to write down as many things as you can think of that might happen if (start timing yourself now and turn the page) . . .

. . . **ALL TELEVISION WAS OUTLAWED**. Start writing *now*.

HOW TO MARK THE TEST

Return to Section One and count up all the words listed in Parts One and Two. Make a note of the score. For Sections Two and Three, simply total up the uses you found for the flower pot and the number of consequences you came up with that might follow if all TV was banned. Add these totals to the first score to produce *one* of the two scores for this test.

Your *second* score is obtained as follows. Look through your answers to Section Two and *place a tick* against any response which fits into one of the following categories:
(1) use of the flower pot as some kind of *container*, i.e. for putting plants in, for holding pencils, knitting needles, paper clips, etc.
(2) use of the flower pot as an instrument of *violence*, i.e. for throwing at the neighbours' cat, drowning mice in, etc.
(3) uses which take advantage of its circular shape, i.e. drawing circles, cutting dough for biscuits, etc.

Now go through the answers for Section Three and *place a tick* against any response which comes into one of the three categories of answer listed below:
(1) those involving changes in personal relationships, i.e. husbands and wives would have more time to talk, people would make more friends, etc.
(2) those which specifically state a substitute activity for watching television, i.e. people would read more books, go to the cinema more often, spend more time in pubs, etc.
(3) those which relate to employment, i.e. newscasters being on the dole, cameramen having to find another job, etc.

Count the ticks and *subtract* this number from your total score for Sections Two and Three. The number remaining, therefore, represents the total of *unticked responses* in these two Sections. Next, you should multiply that total by 5 to obtain your second score on the test. Finally, an overall score is calculated by adding together your *first score and second score*.

For example Score on Section One = 20 points
Number of *unticked* responses on Sections Two and Three = 8
Second score for these two Sections = 40 i.e. (8×5)
Overall score for this test = 60 i.e. $(20 + 40)$

My total score =

WHAT THE TEST TELLS YOU ABOUT YOURSELF

This assessment is designed to measure what is termed 'divergent thinking', a mental ability fundamental to success whenever you are confronted by a problem to which there is no single correct answer. These open-ended questions are in complete contrast to so-called 'convergent' tasks, such as an arithmetic problem or a crossword puzzle, where there is only one way of responding.

Where divergent problems are concerned, there might be a wide variety of equally satisfactory solutions. Furthermore, the answer which finally proves most effective may be reached only after a large number of trial answers have been considered and rejected. Unlike the maths or crossword task where a mistake, like forgetting to 'carry' one or coming up with the wrong word, will lead to confusion and error, it is quite possible to discover the best solution to a divergent question through a series of ideas which only go part of the way to providing the required answer.

Divergent thinking will be employed, for example, when copywriters at an advertising agency are dreaming up a slogan for a new company; when teachers are considering the best methods for helping slow learners, or when scientists are trying to discover the most effective technique for overcoming a research difficulty.

But the role of divergent thinking is much more pervasive than examples given above might suggest. You are just as likely to be confronted with the need to think divergently at home as at work or in school. A couple deciding how to decorate a front room, parents seeking the best way to motivate their child to greater efforts at school, a commuter trying to find the best form of transport through rush-hour traffic are all tackling problems for which there may be many possible – and even a number of equally effective – answers.

It is in areas of creativity, of course, that many of the more subtle divergent problems are to be found; all forms of art, from music through to painting, film direction and theatrical production, demand a high level of divergent thinking ability if they are to be original. A composer, for instance, may be faced with the task of discovering the most aesthetically pleasing succession of musical notes for bringing a cadenza to a close. A novelist may wrestle with the challenge of expressing the personality of his or her characters at a critical point in the story. Artists, confronted with an almost limitless number of visual options, must select the style needed to convey their innermost feelings for the subject.

The study of human creativity has long attracted the attention of psychologists and educators, who have sought to identify the type of thinking involved, discover how it develops and devise ways by which it may be measured. A consistent finding that has emerged from the work is that a major component of creativity is divergent thinking. In a landmark study, Dr. E. Torrance of the United States gave a large group of sixth-formers a test of divergent thinking similar to the one which you have just taken. Seven years later he obtained comprehensive information on a wide range of creative achievements by these young men and women; he found that performance on the original test was highly associated with success in such areas as writing, composing, painting, poetry and original scientific research. In other words, the higher the score on the divergent thinking test, the greater the degree of creativity a person subsequently revealed. To ensure that these successes were maintained, Torrance decided to wait a further five years and take another look at his subjects' achievements before drawing any final conclusions as to the validity of the test. To his surprise he found that, twelve years after those men and women had sat his test, the association between a high score and creative accomplishment was even closer than on the earlier check. Those who had shown a superior ability when responding to questions like those you have just taken actually became *increasingly creative* with the passage of time.

What is the link between creativity and divergent thinking? Research has revealed two principal components of thought essential to any creative activity. The first is a 'fluency factor', which was reflected in your speed scores on the test. This explored your capacity for generating as large a number of responses as possible in a given amount of time. The more answers you thought of throughout the test, the higher your score and the greater your fluency rating. A second key component of creativity is the ability to release any inhibitions to imaginative thinking that may be present and let ideas flow without restraint. Creative thinkers, from Einstein to Picasso, have reported that this is the first and essential stage in the process of solving a problem or the act of creation. During this initial phase the truly creative mind runs, as it were, with the intellectual brake off and the throttle wide open. No attempt is made to censor the outpouring of ideas, even when some of these seem wildly improbable, unlikely or unrealistic. It is only once the imagination has been allowed full and free expression that the second stage in the creative process takes over, as concepts are examined more critically, the obviously unhelpful or unworkable are discarded, and a mental short-list is compiled of those that seem most likely to achieve the required goal.

The creative process is illustrated below in the form of a 'flow-chart', a special type of diagram used when developing computer programs. In a flow chart, each stage of the activity is precisely ordered and the task to be accomplished made explicit.

The ability to generate ideas uninhibitedly was explored from many angles in this test. Section One looked at your talent for making linguistic associations, that is to say, for drawing on your internal vocabulary in order to locate those words which satisfied the conditions stated in Parts One and Two. This is an important ability, since much creative thought is both generated in and expressed by language. Sections Two and Three tested your aptitude for producing a flow of complete ideas rather than simple language associations. Successful performance here depended not only on an ability to use words well but also on forming mental images and making use of other processes of the mind which are not immediately expressible in a verbal form.

Obviously, merely generating a profusion of ideas does not, in itself, result in productive creative thinking. It is not only the quantity but, often more importantly, the quality of those ideas that counts. To assess the originality of the uses which you found for a flower pot and the consequences you imagined for the banning of TV, your second score was derived by *eliminating those responses that are most often mentioned by people taking this type of test*. For instance, when answering the television question, the majority of people talk about changes in social relationships, other leisure activities, and job-loss among TV employees. If you came up with a number of responses that avoided these statistically probable outcomes, then those answers possess greater novelty and originality than the answers commonly produced. An example of a statistically unlikely response is that 'scrap metal dealers' business would increase markedly as the public discarded millions of un-wanted aerials'.

Freshness of ideas is the factor that distinguishes a Picasso or an Einstein from their equally competent but less imaginative colleagues. In order to be an *original* creative thinker, it is essential to avoid re-inventing the wheel!

What your score reveals

43 or less   This is a rather below-average score, but you should not assume that such a result indicates a less-than-able mind. As we have stressed elsewhere in this book, there are many kinds of mental ability, some of which are helpful in particular types of activities while others are needed for different kinds of intellectual work. It may well be that you favour a more convergent approach and find it easier to tackle problems which require a logical progression to a single, correct solution. Your level of aptitude for this kind of challenge is tested elsewhere in this book. Convergent thinking is neither more nor less essential than divergent thinking.

44–59   This is an average score for the test and one which suggests you may be equally at home with both divergent and convergent tasks. Such an aptitude can be helpful since it may mean that you will be able to cope with both convergent and divergent problems with equal ease. Your level of convergent thinking will be tested elsewhere in this book.

Since you already have a moderately good level of divergent ability, you should not encounter too much trouble in developing this skill further by giving yourself further practice on the *same kind of problems* we have used in this test. At least part of the reason for your average score on these questions may be that you have got into the habit of limiting your powers of imagination. You are too prone to censor your thoughts before they can be expressed and so, perhaps, miss out on potentially valuable ideas. Give yourself regular brainstorming sessions in which you throw out all kinds of proposals, either for using everyday objects in an unfamiliar and original manner or by developing notions of what might happen if some highly improbable or even impossible event occurred: water starting to flow uphill, or the ratio of the sexes changing so that there were four times as many men as women in the world!

60 or more This is an above-average score which indicates that you think in a more than usually creative manner, produce highly original ideas and should excel at any mental tasks requiring a divergent approach. In order to decide what kind of occupations or leisure activities are best suited to somebody with such an aptitude, it is necessary to consider what other mental abilities they possess. In the last part of this book we will explain how to bring together all the test results in order to decide what careers or part-time activities most closely match your intellectual prowess. However, as we cautioned at the start, you should resist the temptation to turn to this section until you have completed all nine Assessments, since the results will be more reliable if you take them without being fully aware of what is being assessed.

Leaving aside the question of a specific occupation

or hobby, the test result clearly shows that you have a powerful creative talent which should be allowed satisfactory expression. People like yourself, who are capable of keen original thinking yet unable to exercise this skill in their everyday lives, often experience feelings of dissatisfaction and a desire to gain 'something more' out of life. Whatever the origins of creativity, it appears that the ability includes a psychological drive, which is often very intense, towards its fulfilment. Many potentially creative men and women, however, suppress this drive, for a variety of social or personal reasons. 'I don't have the time' is one common explanation. Others believe that their family or friends will think them 'odd' or 'eccentric' if they take up a secretly yearned-for but rather unconventional or unusual activity. You may have a secret desire for some creative hobby – or even to change your job in order to satisfy your intellectual need for original thought. Forget about the opinions or reactions of others if your creative outlet is unusual in some way. It is *your* intellectual fulfilment which is at stake – not theirs.

To sum up

If you scored above average on this test you are an original, creative thinker whose mental abilities are especially suited to tackling divergent problems – that is, tasks for which there is no single, correct solution.

ASSESSMENT FIVE

This test consists of a special kind of game we call the *XYZ Challenge*. Although simple in concept, you will probably find it quite stimulating mentally, since a complex intellectual skill is being explored.

HOW TO TAKE THIS TEST

In this game, the 'board' is a blank piece of paper and the 'pieces' consist of the letters XYZ. The 'moves' of the game allow you to arrange these letters in horizontal sequences called *strings*. A typical string might, for example, be XXYZXX. These sequences can be varied by adding or changing letters in certain ways, but every move has to be 'legal' in the sense that it satisfies one of four game rules.

Section One contains a series of moves, and your task will be to state whether or not they are legal. In Section Two you will be presented with starting and finishing strings and asked to find the set of legal moves that would transform the first sequence into the final one.

You should begin by reading through the rules and then trying your skill at the practice problems set out below. There is no need to attempt to remember these rules, however, since they will be provided, in abbreviated form, alongside the test questions on each page.

THE RULES OF THE XYZ CHALLENGE

Rule One   END $L_1L_2 : +Y$
If the last two letters of a sequence are *different*, you may add a Y on to the end of that string.
For example: Using this rule, XYZ can be changed into XYZY.

Rule Two   END $2L \rightarrow X$ (the symbol $\rightarrow$ denotes 'can change to')
If a string ends in the *same* two letters, you may substitute an X *in place of* those letters.
For example: By means of this rule, XZZ can be changed into XX.

Rule Three $X\dot{S}X \rightarrow XZX$ ($\dot{S}$ denotes a letter group of any length)
If a group starts and finishes with an X, you may substitute a Z for all the letters between the two Xs.
For example: By using this rule, XZYZZXYZX can be changed into XZXYZX.

Rule Four $L_1L_2 \rightarrow L_2L_1$
Any two *adjacent* letters can change places with each other.
For example: Using this rule, the string XYZ can be written as either XZY (the last two letters switched) or YXZ (the first two letters switched).

These are the only rules and, as mentioned above, they will be repeated in their abbreviated form with each set of problems. Even so, we urge you to spend a few minutes reading through them and working on the practice problems below, so that you fully understand how to play the *XYZ Challenge*.

PRACTICE PROBLEMS

Section One

The next four examples illustrate the type of problems given in Section One of the test, in which your task is to identify any illegal moves. Do this by noting down the letter against the line in which the mistake has been made. In some cases there will not be any errors and you should tick the final statement (d).

Rules

1 END $L_1L_2 : +Y$ 2 END $2L \rightarrow X$ 3 $X\dot{S}X \rightarrow XZX$ 4 $L_1L_2 \rightarrow L_2L_1$

Problem One	*Starting String:* XYZY	
	XYZYY	(a)
	XYZX	(b)
	XX	(c)
	No error	(d)

Problem Two	*Starting String:* XYZ	
	XYY	(a)
	XX	(b)
	X	(c)
	No error	(d)

Problem Three	*Starting String:* ZXXZ	
	ZXZX	(a)
	XZZX	(b)
	XXX	(c)
	No error	(d)

Problem Four	*Starting String:* YYZY	
	YYYZ	(a)
	YYYZY	(b)
	YYYYZ	(c)
	No error	(d)

Section Two

There is one other type of problem that you will encounter. These occur in Section Two and work like this. You are given two strings and are asked to change the first into the second by means of the usual four rules. You are to use one rule at a time in doing this.

Here is a worked example to illustrate how you would proceed.

Problem: change XYZX into XYZYX

This is done as follows: XYZX → XYZXY. (This uses Rule One, which allows you to add a Y when the last two letters are different.) Next you would make the following move in order to complete the task: XYZXY → XYZYX. (This follows Rule Four which enables the positions of the last two letters to be exchanged.) Your sequence of moves would, therefore, be written out as follows:

XYZX

XYZXY

XYZYX

Now try your hand at the following practice problems before you start the test itself. Write out the sequence of moves you decide upon in the form shown above.

Problem Five	*Starting String:* XYZ
	Finishing String: ZXY

Problem Six	*Starting String:* XYX
	Finishing String: XZXY

Problem Seven	*Starting String:* YYYY
	Finishing String: YYXY

Problem Eight	*Starting String:* XYZX
	Finishing String: ZXX

Problem Nine	*Starting String:* XYXX
	Finishing String: ZX

Answers to Practice Problems

Problem One   The illegal move is (c) because the player omitted to write a Z between the two Xs as required by Rule Three.

Problem Two   The illegal move is (a) because Rule One specifies that the Z should have remained in the string.

Problem Three   The illegal move is (c) because, when Rule Three was applied, the middle letter was changed to X when it should have become a Z.

Problem Four   There is no illegal move in this sequence. The moves (a), (b) and (c) conform to Rules Four, One and Four respectively.

Problem Five	*Starting String:* XYZ
	XZY (Rule Four)
	Finishing String: ZXY (Rule Four)

Problem Six	*Starting String:* XYX
	XZX (Rule Three)
	Finishing String: XZXY (Rule One)

Problem Seven	*Starting String:* YYYY
	YYX (Rule Two)
	Finishing String: YYXY (Rule One)

Problem Eight	*Starting String:* XYZX
	XZX (Rule Three)
	Finishing String: ZXX (Rule Four)

Problem Nine   *Starting String:* XYXX
                                          XZX (Rule Three)
                                          ZXX (Rule Four)
                          Finishing String: ZX (Rule Two)

If your answers to any of these problems were incorrect, take some time now to review your understanding of the rules and to identify the cause of your errors. Only proceed to the test itself once you are satisfied you know how to play the *XYZ Challenge*.

SECTION ONE

As explained above, in this Section of the test you must identify illegal moves in the game. This is a timed Section and you must stop writing after exactly 20 minutes. When you are ready to begin, turn the page and start timing yourself.

Rules

1 END L_1L_2 : $+Y$ 2 END $2L \rightarrow X$

3 $X\overset{\cdot}{S}X \rightarrow XZX$ 4 $L_1L_2 \rightarrow L_2L_1$

(1) *Starting String:*   XYZY
XYZYY (a)
XYZX (b)
XX (c)
No error (d)

(2) *Starting String:*   YYYY
YYX (a)
YXY (b)
YY (c)
No error (d)

(3) *Starting String:*   XZYZX
ZZXYX (a)
ZZXZX (b)
ZXZZX (c)
No error (d)

(4) *Starting String:*   XYXYZ
XYYXZ (a)
XYYY (b)
XYX (c)
No error (d)

(5) *Starting String:* YZYXZX
YYZXXZ (a)
YYXZXZ (b)
YXYZXZ (c)
No error (d)

(6) *Starting String:*   YXZZZ
YZXZZ (a)
YZZXZ (b)
YZZXZY (c)
No error (d)

(7) *Starting String:*   XXXXX
XXXZX (a)
XZXZX (b)
XZZZX (c)
No error (d)

(8) *Starting String:*   XYYXY
XYXYY (a)
XYXYX (b)
XZX (c)
No error (d)

(9) *Starting String:*   XYXZXXX
XYXZX (a)
XZXZX (b)
XZX (c)
No error (d)

(10) *Starting String:*   YYXZZ
XXZZ (a)
XZXZ (b)
ZXXZ (c)
ZXXZY (d)
No error (e)

(11) *Starting String:*   XZYXXZX
XZYXZX (a)
XZYXZXY (b)
XYZXZXYY (c)
XZX (d)
No error (e)

(12) *Starting String:* YYYZZZXXX
YYZYZZXXX (a)
YZYYZZXXX (b)
YYZYYZZXXX (c)
YYZYYZZXZX (d)
No error (e)

That is the end of Section One. If you were able to answer all twelve questions, congratulations! If not, don't worry – most people find it impossible to solve the whole set of problems in the time allowed.

Please resist the temptation to turn to the answers and check your solutions until you have completed the set of problems in Section Two. There is *no time limit* on this part of the test, but we advise you to try and finish it in one sitting in order to concentrate your mind on the task. Take a ten-minute rest before proceeding.

SECTION TWO

You will be given starting and finishing strings and asked to work out a series of legal moves to change from one sequence to the other. When you are ready, turn the page and begin. Remember you can take as long as you like over this Section of the test. Even if you cannot get all the way from the first to the last strings, be sure to make a written note of the moves you were able to work out.

Rules

1 END $L_1L_2 : +Y$ 2 END $2L \rightarrow X$ 3 $X\dot{S}X \rightarrow XZX$ 4 $L_1L_2 \rightarrow L_2L_1$

(1)   *Starting String:* ZZX
      Finishing String: XZZ

(2)   *Starting String:* XYXYX
      Finishing String: XZXZX

(3)   *Starting String:* YXX
      Finishing String: YXY

(4)   *Starting String:* XZZZ
      Finishing String: XZXY

(5)   *Starting String:* XYZZ
      Finishing String: XZX

(6)   *Starting String:* XZZXY
      Finishing String: XZX

(7)   *Starting String:* YYXZY
      Finishing String: YXZX

(8)   *Starting String:* YYYY
      Finishing String: X

(9)   *Starting String:* ZYXZZ
      Finishing String: ZX

(10)   *Starting String:* YZXYZX
      Finishing String: YX

(11)   *Starting String:* ZZZZX
      Finishing String: XZZ

(12)   *Starting String:* YZYYZ
      Finishing String: YZZYXY

HOW TO MARK THE TEST

Section One

Check the number of correct solutions using the answer key below. This is your score for Section One.

(1) c (2) c (3) a (4) b (5) a (6) d (7) c (8) b (9) d (10) a (11) c (12) c

Section Two

For each problem, compare your sequence of moves with those provided by the answer key. Award yourself **1 point** for every move that matches one we provide (with the exception of those marked (S) for Starting String). For example, a solution to the problem of changing ZYX to ZYYX might look like this:

	Your solution	*Solution provided by answer key*
	ZYX (S)	ZYX (S)
	ZXY ⎫	
	ZXYY ⎬ *extra steps*	
	ZYXY	ZYXY
		ZYYX

The starting string, ZYX, matches the answer key but the solver receives no points for this since it was given in the test problem. The next two steps (ZXY and ZXYY), though allowable by the rules, are unnecessary and thus have not appeared in the answer key. This means no points should be awarded for them.

Moving on, we notice that the next string (ZYXY) matches a string on the answer key. This allows us to give the sample solution 1 point. Further examination reveals that ZYXY is the last line in the sample solution, indicating that the solver failed to deduce the final string (ZYYX). This means that the solution receives a final total of 1 point.

Remember that the strings with an (S) next to them are not scored.

●   ●   ●

(1) ZZX (S)
    ZXZ
    XZZ

(2) XYXYX (S)
    XZXYX
    XZXZX

(3) YXX (S)
    YX
    YXY

(4) XZZZ (S)
    XZX
    XZXY

(5) XYZZ (S)
    XYX
    XZX

(6) XZZXY (S)
    XZZYX
    XZX

(7) YYXZY (S)
    YXYZY
    YXZYY
    YXZX

(8) YYYY (S)
    YYX
    YXY
    XYY
    XX
    X

(9) ZYXZZ (S)
    ZYXX

There are two ways of proceeding from here.
Both are equally correct:

either ZXYX   *or*   ZYX
       XZYX   ZYXY
       XZX   ZXYY
       ZXX   ZXX
       ZX   ZX

(10) YZXYZX (S)
     YZXZX
     YZZXX
     YZZX
     YZXZ
     YXZZ
     YXX
     YX

(11) ZZZZX (S)
     ZZZXZ
     ZZXZZ
     ZZXX
     ZZX
     ZXZ
     XZZ

(12) YZYYZ (S)

There are two equally correct solutions
to this problem, one more subtle than the
other. If you followed sequence (b) then
award yourself **1 extra point**.

either (a)   YZYZY   *or* (b)   YZYYZY
           YZZYY   YZYZYY
           YZZX   YZZYYY
           YZZXY   YZZYX
          YZZXYY   YZZYXY
          YZZYXY

To obtain an overall score for this test, total the results of Sections One and Two.

My total score =

WHAT THIS TEST TELLS YOU ABOUT YOURSELF

The *XYZ Challenge*, created specially for this book, is what mathematicians term a *formal system*; that is, it consists essentially of a number of symbols (here, the letters X, Y and Z) and precise, specific rules for moving them around in order to create new symbol patterns. Your score, therefore, reveals your aptitude for dealing effectively with such systems by means of an important mental process called *formal reasoning*. What this means in terms of your career prospects and leisure activities will be described in a moment. Let's start, however, by looking at what your score reveals about your aptitude for tasks which demand this type of reasoning.

What your score reveals

less than 20   This is a below-average result and suggests that you may have had some difficulty with activities which call for formal reasoning. It is likely that you find mathematics difficult and are not highly proficient at games like chess or draughts, since these activities are nothing more than formal systems. Many people share your lack of success at this type of thinking, so your low score should not be taken to imply that your mind is somehow inferior to those who obtained a higher score on the test. As we explained in the Introduction, and repeat throughout the book, various intellectual tasks demand very different mental aptitudes. It may well be that your scores on other tests are well above average, indicating that your brain works most efficiently when handling a different type of intellectual challenge.

21–30   This is an average score, indicating a fair level of ability when it comes to manipulating symbols and dealing with the rules of formal systems. You are probably average or somewhat above in mathematical skills and do reasonably well in games such as chess or draughts that demand formal reasoning. With practice, and perhaps greater motivation to tackle formal reasoning tasks, you could probably raise your score quite significantly. If, in the past, you have been attracted to some occupation, training scheme or leisure activity that requires an aptitude for manipulating various kinds of formal systems (such as science, maths, engineering, computer programming, chess, etc.) but doubted your ability to cope with the intellectual demands involved, then your score on this test should help set your mind at rest.

31 or more   This score places you above average for formal reasoning and indicates that you can deal effectively with such systems. What this could imply in terms of work and play are discussed below.

What a high score means in your work

Any occupation which has a strong basis in mathematics or the manipulation of abstract symbols should be ideally suited to your higher-than-average aptitude for formal reasoning.

Because formal systems often function effectively with little or no contribution from language (indeed, it is sometimes necessary to deal with such a system without having any idea what the symbols mean) you do not have to be especially articulate in order to achieve great success.

Let us look more closely at mathematics – a formal system which is the essential starting point for success in a wide variety of scientific and technological subjects. Many mathematicians consider their science to be little more than a formal system whose symbols are manipulated according to carefully derived rules. They feel that maths must be usable even if *no meaning has been assigned to its symbols*.

This may come as a surprise to many lay people who see maths as mainly to do with numbers and essentially practical, being concerned with such mundane tasks as measuring areas or volumes, calculating distances and adding up the grocery bill! Even at a fairly basic level, however, the importance of numbers diminishes considerably, and most maths is concerned with the manipulation of symbols which, in specific contexts, can have numbers substituted for them. Take, for example, the problem:

$$\text{If } ax = y \text{ what does } x \text{ equal?}$$

This is solved by following a simple rule of the 'game' of mathematics which enables us to divide the symbols on both sides of the 'equals sign' by a in order to arrive at a new group of symbols $x = y/a$. Most of higher mathematics proceeds in precisely this way, by the application of exact rules to sets of symbols. Indeed, the great German mathematician David Hilbert asserted that maths is nothing more or less than a game and, as such, every effort must be taken to ensure that its rules do not produce symbol sequences which contradict one another.

Your ability to cope well with formal reasoning suggests that you could become skilled in an occupation currently experiencing a considerable shortage of skilled practitioners: that of the professional mathematician. Industry and science have a great need for *applied mathematics* in which phenomena are carefully observed, the underlying factors considered and a mathematical 'model' created of those facets which seem most significant. Such a 'model' consists of a string, or strings, of symbols, usually in the form of equations, which can be manipulated according to pre-established rules. This enables the modeller to deduce facts about the original phenomenon which would otherwise have gone unnoticed or unconsidered. It is a powerful technique whose value is being increasingly utilized in a wide area of human activities. The engineer, for instance, uses mathematical models to construct bridges and build aircraft; the scientist to formulate theories and make predictions about the outcome of experiments; the businessman to predict the success of a marketing campaign or to minimize the costs of a complex manufacturing process; the physician to determine the rate of malignancy or the spread of a disease. So ubiquitous has this tool become that, without it, our modern technology-based societies simply could not exist.

It may be that exploring ways in which the 'game' of mathematics can be played interests you more than any practical outcomes. In this case you would probably be more attracted to *pure mathematics*, which is concerned solely with the symbols themselves, their rules and their properties. The pure mathematician is content to spend many hours, days, months or even years manipulating symbols, developing new rules and discovering the beautiful hidden subtleties of his craft. This work is no less important than that of the applied mathematician since it not only advances knowledge of the science itself but frequently leads to an application of immense importance and practical benefit in its own right.

Another rapidly expanding area of work, where there is a tremendous demand for highly trained men and women who possess an above-average level of formal reasoning ability, is in the computer industry. The computer itself is no more than an enormously complex formal system whose circuits and interconnections have the sole function of manipulating symbols according to specific rules. Even though such a system shuffles the symbols around with enormous rapidity and can deal with tasks of such complexity they would easily defeat the human brain, its basic form is identical in principle to the simple XYZ game you have just been playing. Programmers relay instructions to their machines by means of highly structured 'languages' consisting of symbols which make sense to the computer only if grouped according to a precise set of regulations. Programmers must learn how to place such symbols in the sequences needed to move from a starting position to the required finishing position without making illegal entries. A high scorer on the XYZ game would be well equipped mentally for a career in this financially and intellectually rewarding field.

Formal thinking and leisure activities

Many popular games are simply formal systems whose symbols are physical objects. In chess for example, a set of symbols – the chess pieces – are moved around according to specific rules. Success depends on being able to plan ahead so as to manoeuvre your pieces into the most favourable positions on the board. You have to work out the sequence of operations needed to achieve this situation, avoiding illegal moves yourself and being on the alert for any made by an opponent. The pieces, and this applies equally to those used in such diverse games as draughts, dominoes, Nim and Go, are purely symbolic, since they possess no meaning outside themselves and their role in that particular game. As such, their status is identical to the symbols of the XYZ game, and your above-average score here indicates that you should be better than most at such leisure activities.

Although all games have rules and often use symbols, in many of them some other element plays a major role in determining who shall win or lose. This additional factor may be pure luck, as in the majority of card games, or physical prowess as in sports such as tennis, squash, snooker, soccer, boxing and the martial arts. Even here, however, your formal reasoning ability could help you excel by allowing you to plan strategies superior to your opponents'. In games which involve a considerable amount of chance, this planning skill will enable you to reduce the odds against you considerably, while in sports – given that you are in good physical condition – you should be able to out-think and outsmart the other players.

Make use of your formal reasoning ability by pursuing leisure activities that place a premium on this kind of intellectual aptitude. Perhaps the test result will encourage you to play chess more seriously, or take up other challenging games; for example, the Japanese game of Go is considered by many to be even more intricate and subtle than chess. You might, equally, think about developing hobbies that are an extension of those activities already discussed under the heading of work. Owning your own microcomputer, for example, and writing programs, just for the pleasure of employing formal reasoning in a practical manner, is often extremely satisfying for anybody with your aptitude.

To sum up

Your high score on this test shows that you can deal effectively with tasks based on a formal system, that is, one in which various kinds of symbols must be manipulated according to specific rules.

ASSESSMENT SIX

HOW TO TAKE THIS TEST

There are no problems to solve or answers to find in this assessment. Instead we want you to carry out a series of tasks which involve the use of pencil, paper and a pair of scissors. It is essential to make copies of these tasks because, in one instance, you have to cut out a design. With this test, however, there is no harm in your seeing the items in advance, so you can make the necessary photocopies yourself.

PART ONE

The object here is to place some dots inside a series of circles. Start with your pencil point resting just *above* the circle labelled S. Note the time, and then, **for exactly 15 seconds**, move around the course in the direction indicated by the arrows, placing a dot inside each of the four circles. In this part of the test, both speed *and* accuracy contribute towards the total score, so remember to work as rapidly and as precisely as you can.

Bear these points in mind:
- dots must be *inside* the circles;
- you must follow the course in the *direction shown by the arrows*;
- you must **stop after 15 seconds**.

When you are ready, place your pencil point above the first circle on page 85, start the time and begin.

PART TWO

This task involves tracing a pencil line through the winding maze shown in the illustration on page 86.

As in Part One, you should time yourself over the course, but on this occasion there is no set limit. The object is to trace a path through the maze quickly and accurately, that is, you should avoid allowing your line to stray across the boundaries while working as rapidly as you possibly can.

Start timing yourself when you begin tracing, and record the time on reaching the end of the maze. Note this time down on a separate sheet of paper. Begin at the point marked S and finish as soon as you reach the letter F.

PART THREE

For this task you will need a photocopy of the illustration on page 87 and a pair of scissors. (A small pair will help you manage the task better.) The object is to cut along the line, starting at the point marked S and finishing at F quickly and accurately, without straying outside the line. Start the timing as you begin to cut, and write down the elapsed time, on a separate sheet of paper, as soon as you reach the end of the line.

PART FOUR

The final task in this assessment is similar to that in Part Two, with one important exception: instead of looking directly at the maze on page 88 while making the tracing, we want you to view it in a mirror. You can do this by using a small (pocket or shaving) mirror and a sheet of cardboard to screen your hand. Position the cardboard over your writing hand so as to prevent yourself from seeing the hand and the paper directly.

The object of this test is to find out how well you can trace a line through the maze while watching the process in a mirror. While looking at the reflection of the maze in the mirror, try to draw a line through the maze starting, as before, at the point marked S. In order for your score to provide a valid indication of your skill on this test, do not remove the cardboard or try to watch your hand directly, but use only the mirror image. Speed and accuracy are equally important but, unlike the other tasks, you will find that considerable care is necessary in order to stay within the maze boundaries. Start timing yourself as you begin and note down the elapsed time immediately on completion.

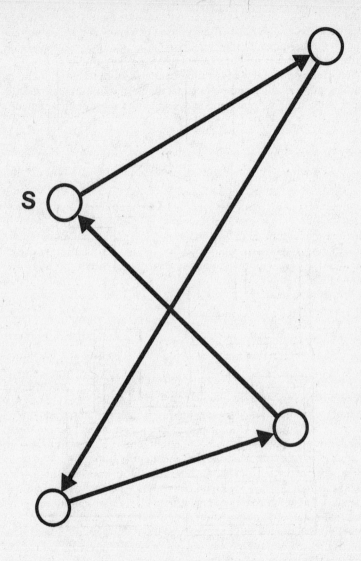

S

Part One

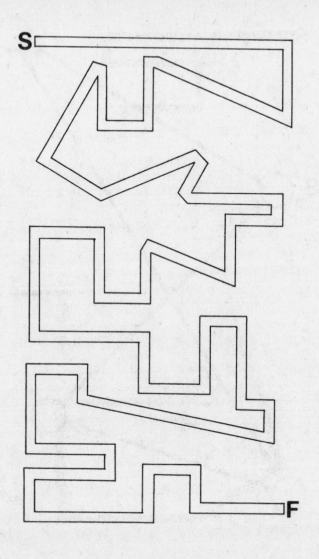

Part Two

Part Three

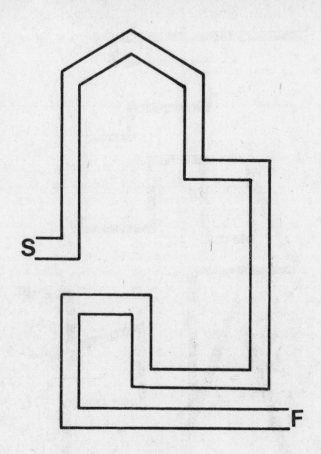

Part Four

HOW TO MARK THE TEST

Both the time and error scores on this assessment are equally important in determining your aptitude for tasks requiring the accurate co-ordination of hand and eye.

Time score

Total your completion times for Parts Two, Three and Four. Next, count the number of dots produced in Part One, *irrespective of whether or not these dots fell inside the circles*. Finally, *subtract* your dot total from the total time on Parts Two, Three and Four. This gives the overall time score on the test. *The lower your score, the faster* you performed. Note this time score on a separate sheet of paper.

Error score

To calculate the *error score*, proceed as follows:
(1) Count the number of dots falling *outside* the circles in Part One.
(2) Add up the number of times your pencil strayed outside the maze boundaries in Part Two.
(3) Total the number of occasions that your scissors cut outside the line in Part Three.
(4) Note the number of times your pencil went outside the maze when doing the mirror drawing test.

Add up these four error scores to provide you with an overall error total. Record this score on a sheet of paper.

My total time score =

My total error score =

WHAT THIS TEST TELLS YOU ABOUT YOURSELF

The chart below will show where your time and error totals place you, by comparison with the population as a whole. Both these scores will be used when interpreting your level of aptitude on this type of task.

What your scores reveal

Errors greater than 20. Speed greater than 68.

Your result is slightly below average. This indicates that you find some difficulty in handling tasks demanding fine hand/eye co-ordination. A low score on this assessment should not be taken to mean that you are clumsy or poorly co-ordinated, however, since a very fine level of skill was being measured here. What it does suggest is that you would be less likely than most to perform successfully on activities demanding subtle control over your hand movements. The occupations and leisure pursuits described below may prove less interesting for you than other activities you could pursue.

Errors: 13–20 Speed: 56–68

Your scores on these tasks are average; this suggests that you can cope reasonably well with any activities demanding fine co-ordination between hand and eye. You should be able to perform reasonably well in the activities and leisure pursuits described below.

Errors less than 12. Speed less than 55.

Your scores on this assessment are above average, indicating a high level of aptitude on tasks demanding fine hand and eye co-ordination. You should be able to perform well in the occupations and leisure pursuits described below.

Your time and error scores might also be used to place you in one of two specific categories:

If your time score was more than 64 and your error total less than 12, you are a **Slow-Accurate Performer**.

If your time score was less than 64 and your error total under 12, then you are a **Fast-Accurate Performer**.

As you will realize, the ability to co-ordinate hand and eye movements accurately and quickly has an important bearing on one's performance in, and enjoyment of, a wide range of occupations and leisure-time activities.

The Fast-Accurate Performer

Your scores indicate you work rapidly and with precision on tasks demanding efficient use of your hands. This suggests that you will tackle manual tasks with speed, yet manage to produce a careful and thorough job. You can undertake most types of fine work with confidence, making fewer false starts and a smaller number of errors than your less efficient colleagues. Your nimble fingers should stand you in good stead in any hobby or job demanding precise use of the hands.

In your work
Fine hand/eye co-ordination is a prerequisite for success in such a wide range of occupations that it would be impossible to list them all here. They range from surgery, especially the microsurgical techniques used in eye operations, dental work or neurosurgery, to assembly-line work.

As we have stressed throughout this book, results on one assessment are obviously insufficient to determine an individual's best career choice. What can be said with confidence, however, is that if the job demands your working rapidly but precisely with your hands, then this result indicates you should do well on this aspect of the job at least.

In your leisure time
Any hobby or pastime which requires good co-ordination should prove well suited to your special aptitude for fine, fast work. You might, for instance, consider magic, since sleight-of-hand demands extremely nimble fingers and much of the apparatus used is small and intricate. Other hobbies where fine fast hand/eye co-ordination is essential include juggling, playing musical instruments, and every pursuit that requires you to manipulate things. Other possibilities you might find interesting are model-making, building intricate electronic equipment, painting miniatures, engraving and tying fish flies.

It is also probable that you would be successful in manual activities in which the product constructed undergoes rapid transformations from one state to another. For example, the potter's wheel would soon become a good friend to you. In pottery, furniture-making, metal crafts, to name a few, the craftsman has to make instantaneous moment-to-moment decisions about how to change pressure, angle, and other factors as an object he is creating takes shape before his eyes. This is the sort of manual speed and accuracy that your test results indicate you possess.

Surprisingly, a fast-accurate performance on tasks which demand hand/eye co-ordination and efficiency does not necessarily indicate superior athletic performance, since success there primarily demands control over the larger muscles. It appears that different systems are involved in gross and fine-motor performance.

The Slow-Accurate Performer

The result of the assessment suggests that you prefer to take your time over manual tasks in order to ensure that things are done as accurately as possible. You have a high degree of concentration when using your hands and will spend long periods of time on fine work. You probably value fine workmanship in the products you buy and own, feeling that, whenever possible, it is worth paying extra for high quality.

In your work

Craftsmanship is the keynote of performance so far as you are concerned. You would be unhappy in any occupation where you could not devote sufficient time to do each job carefully and precisely. You would be most at home, and be using your manual skills to best advantage, in some craft industry where the emphasis was on getting things done right rather than in the shortest possible time. In the professions you should try to work in an area where it is financially possible to spend time in getting the job done as close to perfection as possible. As a dentist or dental technician, for example, you might well be happier dealing with private patients rather than having to compromise your skills by working against the clock. Avoid any manual occupations where the final say in how much care and effort goes into a particular product lies with somebody else, because this could well lead to stressful confrontations as your desire for perfection comes into conflict with output quotas.

In your leisure time

Fine modelling of ships, planes, trains; antique restoration; painting miniatures, constructing small items of electronic equipment; creating working replicas . . . all these are pursuits in which the slow-accurate performer excels.

To sum up

This assessment explored manual skills involving the accurate co-ordination of hand and eye. If you are a fast-accurate performer then you will be best suited to any job demanding rapid but precise manipulation of objects. If you are a slow-accurate performer, go for occupations and leisure pursuits which allow you to express your ability as a craftsman with an eye – and a hand – for fine details.

ASSESSMENT SEVEN

HOW TO TAKE THIS TEST

In this assessment you will be asked to study a series of designs and line drawings and to state your preferences among them. Starting on the next page there are a series of picture problems. Each consists of either three similar designs or three line drawings all showing the same scene from a slightly different perspective. All you have to do is decide which of the three you prefer and make a note of its identification number (1, 2 or 3) on a separate sheet of paper. There is no time limit on the test, but avoid spending too long on any particular item. The most valuable response, from the point of view of assessing your artistic abilities, is the one which springs to mind almost immediately.

PART ONE

When you are ready to make a start turn the page . . .

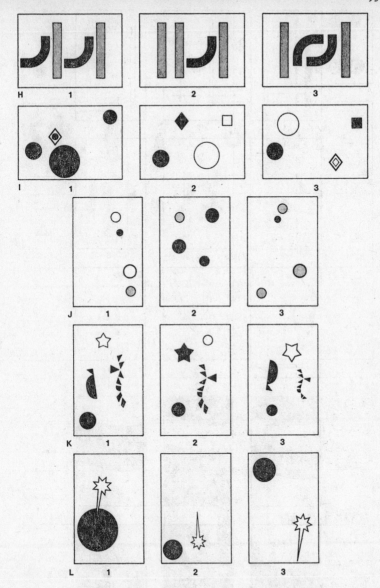

H 1   2   3

I 1   2   3

J 1   2   3

K 1   2   3

L 1   2   3

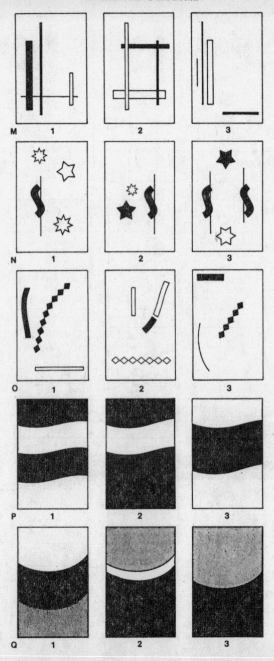

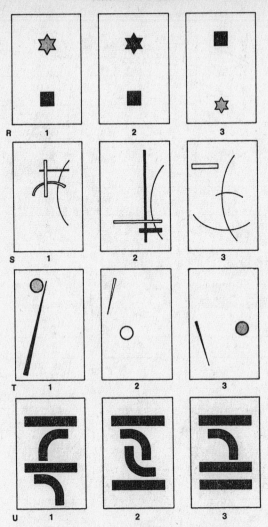

R   1   2   3

S   1   2   3

T   1   2   3

U   1   2   3

PART TWO

When you are ready to make a start turn the page . . .

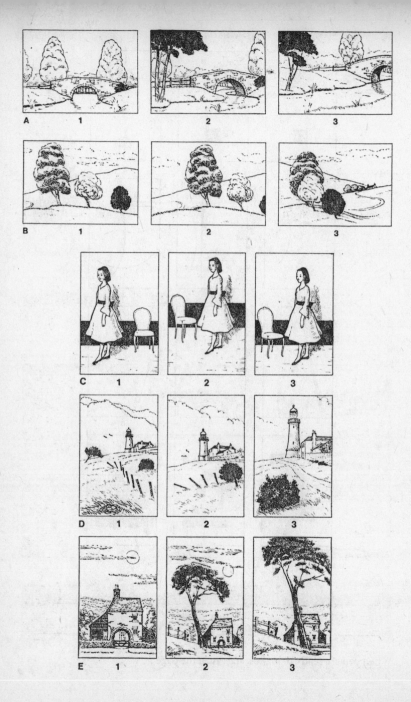

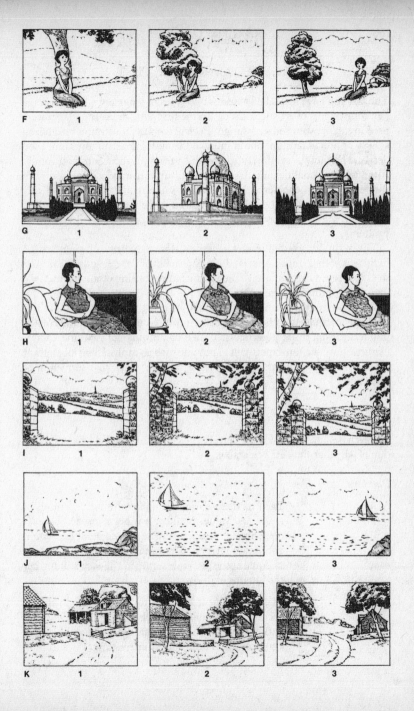

HOW TO MARK THE TEST

The test you have just taken assesses two types of judgment which form the key components of artistic aptitude. In the first part, geometric shapes were used to explore your sense of design. Each of the three illustrations contained a 'best' option in terms of one or more of the most important aspects of good design, harmony, symmetry, balance, variety, proportion and unity. Although such qualities are, to some extent, subjective and vary according to the 'eye of the beholder', there are still some motifs which are clearly preferable to others and would be so judged by people with natural artistic aptitude, whether or not they happened to be professional designers or painters.

The second part of the test measured the soundness of your artistic judgment of *composition*, that is, the arrangement of the elements in a picture so as to create a harmonious whole in which the more important features of a scene are appropriately emphasized.

Check your answers on this assessment by using the key below. You will also find an explanation as to why Richard Armstrong, the artist who created this test for us, made a particular design or drawing his own first choice. Naturally, we did not expect you to provide such an explanation; all that was needed here was your first impression of the illustration that seemed most pleasing.

Answer Key

For each design or drawing the correct choice is accompanied by an explanation of why that choice is preferable.

Part One

A   2   Each of these designs is unified by the repetition of shape and value. Number 2 is better unified because of dominant area, dominant area contrast and dominant space interval. The variety achieved by the use of unequal space intervals serves to enhance still further the interest of design 2.

B   3   The arrangement of the three unequal shape differences creates a contrast which is more interesting than in the other two. The unequal spaces between shapes also makes this design more interesting.

C	1	Unity here is achieved through the dominance of the triangle, the use of value (grey shading) and space interval.
D	3	The only design which creates harmony and unity leading to a feeling of wholeness.
E	2	Here, as in the design above, harmony has been achieved. The fact that it takes only small design changes to disrupt such harmony is well shown by the minor modifications to Number 3.
F	1	Has formal balance, with dominance produced by both size and repetition.
G	3	Here the design is balanced by contrast of direction with the dominant left oblique in harmony with short sides of the surrounding rectangle. This reinforcement of the vertical short sides prevents them from being overpowered by the horizontals, producing a stronger and more interesting contrast of direction.
H	2	The best choice because of dominance of one kind of line (straight) and unification created by one dominant value (grey).
I	1	This design has a dominant *shape* (round), dominant *size* (large disc) and dominant *value* (black). The interval between the large and small discs provides a dominant space interval.
J	3	Balance here has been achieved through the use of one dominant value and a contrasting space interval.
K	2	The dominance of three basically round shapes over the one asymmetrical shape gives this design the greatest harmony.
L	1	Balance in this design is better than in the other two because the elements have been positioned more effectively. Greater unification has been achieved through the dominance of one of two contrasting shapes. More interest is also produced through the contrast of dark and light areas, where the shapes touch, and between the angle and curve.

M	I	This design has the greatest variety and unity, and the best balance. There are contrasting values with black dominating. The variety of spacing also contributes to this design's success.
N	I	Here we have four different elements in which three have been combined to form a dominant group; three white to one black, three symmetrical to one asymmetrical, three round to one long. These designs are similar to those shown in K, above, but with the addition of value.
O	I	This design contains a dominance of curved line and zig-zag. Black dominates white and non-straight lines predominate, with the zig-zag being strongest.
P	2	Here unity of value (black) is achieved by dominance of area, and the most successful balance of the three designs achieved through variety of size and shapes.
Q	2	This is the most interesting due to the use of size and shapes of different values. Black dominates, whereas, in the other designs, the values have equal proportions.
R	I	The dominant black square creates stronger value against background contrast than the grey circle. Number 3 has the same contrast, but the arrangement of the two elements is weaker. In Number 2, both shapes are equally strong so that dominance is absent, with each shape struggling for the viewer's attention.
S	2	This is the best design for reasons similar to those stated in M above. Here, in addition, straight is nicely opposed to curved, vertical contrasts with horizontal, thick lines with thin, and black is opposed to white.
T	I	This design shows how value contrast can emphasize line and direction. Unity is produced through the dominance of the oblique straight line.
U	3	The design is unified by the dominance of straight lines. The other two lack such unity and so appear unresolved with all the elements struggling for dominance.

Part Two

A 2 In Number 1, the apparently pleasing symmetry of the scene turns out to be a visual prison. The eye, having been drawn under the bridge, is then given nowhere to go. In Number 3, the arch of the bridge has been interrupted, so that the eye is held at the river's edge and the line of the bank is very dull. By stepping back and to one side, as in Number 2, the river gently leads the eye under the bridge and gives room for the imagination to wander. The arch of the bridge then leads the eye back into the picture to the trees on the left and the viewer can start again.

B 3 Number 1 has two contrasting diagonals, the distant hill and the descending height of the trees. As a result, each tree sings a solo. In Number 2, the too large central tree is excessively dominant, while the winding lane directs the gaze out of the picture. In Number 3, the lane takes the eye to a point of visual interest, while the sweeping curves of the land produce a harmonious whole.

C 3 In Number 1, the figure is too close to the left-hand frame and the direction of the gaze, being to the left, takes the viewer's eye out of the picture. In Number 2, the subject's head is uncomfortably close to the top of the frame, producing a stifling absence of psychological space; in the third drawing, the figure is placed to the right of centre and, by gazing left, leads the viewer's eye into the drawing.

D 1 The first drawing works best because the lines of direction, fence to tree, tree to lighthouse along the horizon, lighthouse to bush and back to fence, take the eye on a visually exciting journey. The rest provides foreground interest, and the sky area an interesting background. Number 2 is less satisfactory because of the central position of the lighthouse tower, a lack of foreground interest and the fact that the line of fence leads the eye out of the picture while dividing the ground too evenly. Number 3 is dull because of the central position of the tower and the fact that both road and horizon take the eye on a journey to nowhere.

E   2   Proportions in Number 1 are bad with an equal amount
                of earth and sky being shown. This uninspiring
                balance is lent further emphasis by the top of the
                cottage roof. The second choice is the best balance,
                since the earth, sky, and other features have been
                placed in pleasing relations to one another. Number 3
                is too clever. The moon is lost in the tree, the cottage
                has been spoiled by the trunk and the eye is taken too
                high in the frame by the tree.

F   3   The third drawing is a very well balanced scene with
                good use made of space. The first is a compositional
                cliché, with the tree growing out of the figure. Number
                2 is slightly more acceptable, but here the figure
                merges with the foliage. The chief fault, however, is
                the poor use of space. The right hand half of the scene
                contributes very little. You can prove this for yourself
                by covering that part of the picture. You will find that
                the composition works fairly well without it.

G   1   Formal balance is achieved in Number 1 and there is no
                treatment as satisfactory as this rather trite viewpoint
                for demonstrating the perfect symmetry of this and
                other architectural gems. (This series is a trap for
                people who dismissed the first drawing using the same
                arguments used in A above. The other two drawings
                prove the point. Care has to be taken to include in the
                finished work all the elements which produce sym-
                metry in the subject.)

H   1   Number 1 provides an elegant composition with the
                head *just* off centre, dividing background space in an
                interesting manner. This division occurs in Number 2
                as well, but now the picture as a whole seems unba-
                lanced and the eye tends to run out of the frame at the
                bottom right-hand corner. The plant has equal emph-
                asis with the figure, creating a further imbalance, in
                Number 3. Since the figure is gazing out to the right in
                this picture, it is a mistake to place her too far to the
                right.

I   2   Number 1 is almost acceptable, as the gateposts neatly
                frame a pleasant view and the ratio of earth to sky is

pleasing. By looking at the same view from slightly further back, however, the same scene is greatly enhanced with branches and foliage. In Number 3, the same principle has been applied but overdone; the one-to-one ratio of earth and sky makes the image a dull one, but the greatest loss is any base to the picture.

J   1   Foreground rocks provide a solid base from which to view the scene in Number 1, and add interest. The two-thirds-sky formula is one often employed by the Old Masters. The placing of the boat is most satisfactory in this position. Try mentally putting it anywhere else in the drawing and you will prove the point. In Number 2, the two-thirds-sea/sky balance is maintained, but now the boat is too far to the left and the view unbalanced as a result. In Number 3, the picture is not only hopelessly unbalanced but the proportion of sea to sky is too equal and this makes the picture uninteresting.

K   2   Number 1 may look pleasant enough at a glance, but you quickly discover that the lower third is uninteresting while the road is too central and leads nowhere. In Number 3, the entire centre strip, from top to bottom, has almost no visual interest, with the road taking the eye nowhere except to a graphic anti-climax! This makes Number 2 the best choice, as the wider view introduces more foreground interest and the eye is led into the drawing by the road.

The table below will show you where your total score on the assessment, obtained by adding the total correct answers in Parts One and Two of the test, places you in relation to the rest of those who took the test.

My Total Score =

Where your results place you

Score	0–9	10–14	15–24
Your Standing	below average	about average	above average

WHAT THIS TEST TELLS YOU ABOUT YOURSELF

A high level of artistic aptitude enables you to choose a range of occupations and leisure pursuits far wider than painting pictures or creating sculptures. If you achieved more than 15 points on Part One, there are numerous activities – both part-time and full-time – you might want to consider taking up. As a hobby, you could attend evening classes on pottery, ceramics, jewellery, floral, fashion, fabric or furniture design. Any of these could lead to a career which, when successful, can prove highly profitable. The fact that you have a good eye for design does not, of course, constitute any guarantee that such success will be forthcoming, but at least you have the ability to understand and create good designs.

This flair is also an essential attribute in a number of leisure and work areas that might not, at first sight, appear to involve anything 'artistic'. For instance, graphic reproduction in the printing industry involves making letterpress illustration 'blocks', lithographic printing plates and stencils for screen printing. This involves some of the most interesting and difficult work found in the printing industry, combining a technical knowledge of photography – negatives and plates of the illustrations are produced in all these processes – and an artistic skill in retouching the plates before printing can take place. Design skills of a high order are also called upon in blazoning (depicting according to the rules of heraldry) armorial bearings for families with a right to display their coat of arms. Less traditional, but no less skilful, is the creation of modern-day heraldic devices, the logos employed by companies to identify themselves and their products.

If you scored above 8 points on Part Two, then you have have an above-average eye for pictorial composition and might consider a hobby or career where this aptitude could be put to best use. If you also have a sound drawing ability then you might take up painting, illustrating, graphic design, sketching or sculpture, either as an absorbing leisure activity or as a full-time occupation.

A lack of drawing skill need not deter you from other forms of artistic expression where the ability to compose effectively is equally essential, for instance in photography. Having a good 'eye for a picture' is an essential attribute for all camera operators, whether professional or amateur, even in areas of work which may seem far removed from artistry in the classical sense. News and magazine photographers, for example, try hard to achieve strong and compelling compositions, even when working under conditions of great hardship and hazard. If you examine the work of internationally respected war cameramen, such as Robert Capa, Eugene Smith, Larry Burrows or even Matthew Brady who covered the American Civil War using a cumbersome plate camera, you will find that their sense of composition is powerful and direct, compelling attention from the viewer. Even in the far more mundane world of studio photography, where the subject may be no more exotic or exciting than a collection of pots and pans being photographed for use by a mail-order catalogue, an instinctive understanding for the requirements of composition is essential.

An above-average ability is also helpful in such diverse occupations as architecture, interior design, landscape gardening, creating window displays, theatrical and film design, and scenic model building.

If you attained an above-average score on both parts of this assessment, you have considerable artistic aptitude and could put it to use in a wide variety of ways.

In your work

Some of the more obvious careers demanding artistic ability have already been described. In addition, you could consider dealing in fine art and *objets d'art* as your above-average talent for design and composition would enable you to appreciate the subtleties of the objects you handle and you would be able to exercise good judgement about them, once sufficient background had been gained in this field.

Interior decorating could be another area where your aptitude for assessing both composition and design would be put to good effect. If you also have an eye for colour and the ability to match colours, you might be extremely successful in designing interiors for homes, offices and shops, creating sets for the film, TV and advertising industries, acting as an adviser on the purchase of furnishings, carpets, curtains and wallpaper.

In your leisure

Many of the professions and careers outlined above can also become absorbing and often financially rewarding, part-time pursuits. Whatever you choose, find an interest that allows you to take full advantage of this fairly rare and very valuable skill.

To sum up

If you obtained an above-average score on Part One, you have a good eye for design and should consider a work or leisure-time activity that takes advantage of this aptitude. A score that is higher than average in Part Two indicates a superior eye for composition, which could prove of great benefit not only in the more obvious artistic activities but in many related fields. If you scored above average on both parts of this assessment then you combine a flair for design with an artist's eye for composition.

ASSESSMENT EIGHT

HOW TO TAKE THIS TEST

There is no time limit on this assessment which may, if you wish, be completed in more than one session. Your task is to improve a series of sentences, in some instances simply by deleting unnecessary words, on other occasions by replacing a few of them with more appropriate ones. Use the examples below to check that you understand what is required before starting on the assessment proper.

SAMPLE SENTENCES

(1) I do not wish to prolong the course of this meeting.
(2) At this point in time I want to outline my proposals.
(3) The scientist checked her results again to make doubly certain no mistakes would occur.

Now stop for a moment and write an edited version of each on a piece of scrap paper. When you have done this check your versions with those given below.

Answers

(1) I do not wish to prolong ~~the course of~~ this meeting.

Here the phrase *the course of* is superfluous because it contributes nothing to the clarity of the idea expressed. The deletion of the phrase improves the flow of words without changing the sense of the text.

(2) ~~At this po/nt in time~~ Now I want to outline my proposals.
   or:
   ~~At this point in time~~ I/now want to outline my proposals.

Correct editing here requires a deletion of five words and their replacement by the single word 'now'. Both corrected versions are equally satisfactory and would merit the same number of points when scoring. But you would have lost marks if your version had included *only* the deletion since, without the addition of 'now', the sense of the text is altered.

(3) The scientist checked her results again to ~~make doubly/certain no~~ ^{avoid} mistakes ~~would occur~~.

Replacing those six words by 'avoid' greatly improves the flow of the sentence. Be on the lookout in the test for similar instances of needlessly wordy texts.

In no case do you need to rewrite any of the sentences *completely*.

If your grasp of English usage is fairly basic, do not feel that you are bound to do badly at this assessment. It is quite possible to obtain a better-than-average score on the test without having a deep knowledge of sentence structure and the rules of English grammar. Provided you possess a sufficient 'feel' for words and have an aptitude for identifying a clumsy sentence construction or an awkward turn of phrase, you could still do well. Many people who lack a formal training in English can edit sentences successfully without being able to specify exactly *why* certain words were used wrongly or why particular sentences were needlessly confused . . . This is all we ask of you here. In the answer section an explanation will be provided, telling you why one version of a sentence is better than another; but you are not expected to explain your reasons for making particular changes in the test. All you need worry about is crossing out words which seem not to belong and, on many occasions, replacing them with more appropriate ones.

Now it is your turn to don the green eye-shade, sharpen your correcting pencil and place yourself in the editing chair. Since considerable work will have to be done on the sentences below, you should photocopy the pages or write your corrected texts on a separate sheet of paper to avoid marking the book.

----

(1) This type and kind of behaviour will not be tolerated.

(2) Prior to the start of the meeting, he carefully arranged his notes.

(3) I believe that this is rather impossible.

(4) She was under compunction to finish the report by 5 p.m.

(5) In the instances where your obligations are neglected, you will be fined.

(6) He joined the ends of the rope together and tugged gently.

(7) Please initiate the operation of the timer.

(8) By means of writing quickly, he took down everything they said.

(9) In regard to the students they have all received full funding for their research.

(10) I am opposed to any moves that would extend the duration of the conflict.

(11) This is an example of highly correct behaviour.

(12) As you know her, you had better go.

(13) You should now proceed to the window on the left.

(14) I have heard that his release is eminent and that he is in good physical health.

(15) While he never seemed worried about the bills, he did make immediate arrangements to pay them.

(16) The condition of this car is quite perfect; I will buy it.

(17) As a rule, we usually close at five and everyone leaves.

(18) This sort of opinion is almost universal.

(19) I am concerned about the question as to whether or not your plans to purchase the new factory will be accepted by the other members of the board.

(20) The plane took off and quickly disappeared from sight.

(21) He replied with a crude and somewhat obvious pun.

(22) His spasmodic attempts at work occurred in fits and starts.

(23) I wish to stress the point that the trucks in your fleet require frequent servicing.

(24) There are two reasons for not proceeding: in the first place we cannot afford it and second it is of no use.

(25) Why don't I go? The reason is simply because I choose not to.

(26) The side's supporters were few in number and always silent.

(27) We must take appropriate measures to stem this rebellion and regain control.

(28) Sporadic outbreaks of firing occurred. They were scattered and elicited an immediate response from our soldiers.

(29) If and when I get permission to change the filing system, I shall act accordingly.

(30) Plainclothes detectives approached the area from several adjacent side streets and intermingled with the crowd.

(31) After carefully ruminating upon the matter, it is my considered opinion that the changes you recommend will in all probability have to be delayed.

(32) More of our citizens seem to be immigrating from our shores.

(33) They had an absolutely superb day at the races because the weather was completely perfect.

(34) We wish to advise you that your order of 22 June will be dispatched within the next seven days.

(35) I found that his prejudices were extremely aggravating.

(36) It was not surprising that she had difficulties in her studies, because the doctors later discovered her to be a deaf and dumb person.

(37) I doubt that there is a more devoted subject of Her Majesty than the officer you so ridicule.

(38) Thanks to our efforts, we have found that less than ten new cases of the disease were reported annually.

(39) The great ship, stranded on the beach near the town, certainly presented an intriguing sight.

(40) The science-fiction writer made many futuristic comments about tomorrow, but I doubt whether he will be proved correct.

HOW TO MARK THE TEST

Compare your edited versions of the sentences with the answers below. Award yourself 1 **point** for each word crossed out on your copy *which has also been deleted in our text*. A further **point** can be given for each word *you added to the sentences* which corresponds to one in the answers.

An example should make the scoring system clear. If you look at sentence (27), you will see that our edited version reads:

act
We must ~~take appropriate measures~~ to stem this rebellion and regain control.

Suppose you had edited the sentence to read:

We must take ~~appropriate~~ measures to stem this rebellion and regain control.

This would have been worth just *one point*, for the deletion of 'appropriate'. To obtain the maximum possible marks on this sentence you should have deleted three words and replaced them by one word, a possible total score of *four points*.

Answers

(The number in brackets after each sentence indicates the maximum possible score. Total your marks to provide an overall score for the assessment.)

(1) This ~~type and kind of~~ behaviour will not be tolerated. (4)

The additional words are superfluous to the meaning of the sentence.

Before
(2) ~~Prior to the start of~~ the meeting, he carefully arranged his notes. (6)

This is needlessly wordy. The deletion makes the sentence more concise.

(3) I believe that this is ~~rather~~ impossible. (1)

A thing may be either possible or impossible, it cannot be *rather* impossible.

obliged *or* required
(4) She was ~~under compunction~~ to finish the report by 5 p.m. (3)

Incorrect use of the word compunction which really means 'remorse' or 'uneasiness resulting from wrongdoing'.

If
(5) ~~In the instances where~~ your obligations are neglected, you will be fined. (5)

Bureaucrats in particular are fond of using several words when one will serve much better. This change makes the meaning clearer at first reading.

(6) He joined the ends of the rope ~~together~~ and tugged gently. (1)

Since he *could* only join the ends 'together', the word is superfluous.

(7) Please ~~initiate the/operation of~~ the timer. (5)
^{start}

Needless use of words which should be edited out.

(8) By ~~means of~~ writing quickly, he took down everything they said. (2)

No need to retain those extra words, since they contribute nothing to the clarity of meaning.

(9) ~~In regard to t~~he students ~~they~~ have all received full funding for their research. (4)
^{The}

More unnecessary words to be struck out.

(10) I am opposed to any moves that would ~~extend the/ duration of~~ the conflict. (5)
^{lengthen}

'extend the duration of' is unnecessarily wordy.

(11) This is an example of ~~highly~~ correct behaviour. (1)

If the behaviour is correct, it cannot be any more correct.

(12) ~~As~~ you know her, you had better go. (2)
^{Since *or* because}

'As' cannot be used as an alternative to 'because' or 'since', either of which is the correct word to use here.

(13) You should now ~~proceed~~ to the window on the left. (2)
^{go}

A more concise way of saying the same thing.

(14) I have heard that his release is ~~eminent~~ and that he is in good physical health. (2)
^{imminent}

Those two words are often confused. 'Eminent' means either 'prominent' or, in the sense of personal attainment, 'distinguished'.

(15) ~~While~~ he never seemed worried about the bills, he did make immediate arrangements to pay them. (2)
^{Although *or* Though}

Incorrect use of 'while'. The sense intended here clearly demands the use of 'although' or 'though'.

(16) The condition of this car is ~~quite~~ perfect; I will buy it. (1)

As with 'impossible', perfection is an absolute value that cannot be qualified.

(17) ~~As a rule~~ we usually close at five, and everyone leaves. (3)

They either close at five 'as a rule' or they 'usually' close at five; it is not possible to do both. This would be the same as saying: 'I always do that usually . . .' Since it is unlikely that any strict rule compels them to close at five, the writer presumably meant to tell us that on most occasions work was over by five. So we can delete the 'as a rule' bit and leave in 'usually'. If, however, something else in the sentence told us that work really did always stop on the dot of five in accordance with some strictly enforced regulation, then it would be correct to say: 'As a rule we close at five . . .' However, given the sense of the text our version seems the most probable. If you edited it to 'As a rule we close . . .' however, you can award yourself one point.

(18) This sort of opinion is ~~almost~~ ~~universal~~ widely held. (4)

It is either 'universal' or it is not; as with 'perfect' and 'impossible', you cannot qualify the term. The intention is conveyed by the use of 'widely held'.

(19) I am concerned about ~~the question as to~~ whether ~~or not~~ your plans to purchase the new factory will be accepted by the other members of the board. (6)

Redundancy again. Editing out these words makes the sense clearer and the sentence more concise.

(20) The plane took off and quickly disappeared ~~from sight~~. (2)

Redundancy. It could not have disappeared from anything but sight!

(21) He replied with a crude and ~~somewhat~~ obvious pun. (1)

'Somewhat' is a word which often slips into speech and writing without any good reason. Here, it is to some extent self-contradictory.

(22) His ~~spasmodic~~ attempts at work occurred in fits and starts. (1)

Since 'spasmodic' means 'in fits and starts', the word is redundant.

(23) I wish to stress ~~the point~~ that the trucks in your fleet require frequent servicing. (2)

Not required for either clarity or emphasis, so delete.

(24) There are two reasons for not proceeding: ~~in the first place~~ we cannot afford it, and ~~second~~ it is of no use. (5)

No useful purpose is served by using the phrase 'in the first place' and 'second'.

(25) Why don't I go? ~~The reason is~~ Simply because I choose not to. (3)

'Choosing' not to go is obviously a reason, so there is no need to describe it as such.

(26) The side's supporters were few ~~in number~~ and always silent. (2)

They could not be few in anything but number! Redundancy yet again.

act
(27) We must ~~take~~ appropr~~iate measures~~ to stem this rebellion and regain control. (4)

Never use more words than you need to make your point clearly and exactly.

produced
(28) Sporadic outbreaks of firing occurred. They ~~were scattered and elicited~~ an immediate response from our soldiers. (5)

'Scattered' is redundant, since we already know they were sporadic. 'Elicited' can mean to evoke a response from somebody, but sounds rather pompous. 'Produced' is a more acceptable word in this context.

(29) If ~~and when~~ I get permission to change the filing system, I shall
do so
~~act/accordingly~~. (6)

The phrase 'if and when' is often used unnecessarily. The words 'if' and 'when' can be used exclusively, the former to express doubt: 'If I get permission. . .', the latter to take something for granted: 'When I get permission . . .'. Here the writer clearly wishes to express some doubt that permission will be forthcoming and the when is unnecessary; 'act accordingly' is somewhat pompous and better replaced by 'do so'.

(30) Plainclothes detectives approached the area from several ~~adjacent~~ side
mingled
streets and inter~~mingled~~ with the crowd. (3)

'Adjacent' is unnecessary, since they would have to be close by; 'mingled' describes what happened more simply.

considering *or* thinking over   I believe
(31) After carefully ~~ruminating upon~~ the matter ~~it is my considered opinion~~
probably
that the changes you recommend will ~~in all probability~~ have to be delayed. (14)

Clarify the ideas by using a minimum of words which express your meaning most directly and exactly.

emigrating
(32) More of our citizens seem to be ~~immigrating from our shores~~. (5)

'Emigration' (leaving a country) and 'immigration' (entering a new one) are often confused. Since emigration means 'leaving one's native shores', the last three words are redundant.

a
(33) They had ~~an absolutely~~ superb day at the races because the weather was ~~completely~~ perfect. (4)

Further examples of a failure to allow words which describe the highest degree of completeness or perfection to stand on their own.

inform *or* let you know
(34) We wish to ~~advise~~ you that your order of 22 June will be dispatched within the next seven days. (2)

The word 'advise' is often found in business letters. However, used in this way it is incorrect.

irritating *or* annoying
(35) I found that his prejudices were extremely ~~aggravating~~. (2)

Contrary to popular belief, 'aggravate' does not mean to 'annoy' or 'irritate', the sense in which it is used here; it means 'to make something worse or more serious', as in: 'The strike will aggravate our critical cash-flow problems.'

(36) It was not surprising that she had difficulties in her studies, because the

mute
doctors later discovered her to be a deaf ~~and dumb person~~. (4)

To call somebody 'a deaf and dumb person' is incorrect. Deaf mute is the proper description, but 'discovered her to be deaf and dumb' would be acceptable. Award 4 points if you have used the latter.

if
(37) I doubt ~~that~~ there is a more devoted subject of Her Majesty than the officer you so ridicule. (2)

What the writer presumably meant to say was that no other officer was as devoted. What he actually said cast doubt on the officer's devotion.

fewer
(38) Thanks to our efforts, we have found that ~~less~~ than ten new cases of the disease were reported annually. (2)

Confusions of this kind are common. 'Less' is concerned with extent, volume or bulk; 'fewer' has to do with number. So we have 'less sunshine' in winter and 'fewer people' on the beaches.

(39) The great ship, stranded on the beach near the town, certainly presented
    interesting *or* exciting
an ~~intriguing~~ sight. (2)

'Intriguing' cannot be used in this way because it means 'plotting to achieve some goal by secret strategies'. It does not mean that something is 'exciting' or 'interesting', although people mistakenly use it in this way.

(40) The science-fiction writer made many ~~futuristic~~ comments about tomorrow, but I doubt whether he will be proved correct. (1)
'Futuristic' cannot be applied to comments, only to trends in art. The way it is used here is therefore incorrect; it is also redundant, since comments concerning 'the future' – which the writer obviously meant to imply – must logically be about things happening 'tomorrow'!

Add up your score and then look at the chart below to see what this reveals about your aptitude for expressing yourself clearly and accurately in written English.

My total score =

WHAT THIS TEST TELLS YOU ABOUT YOURSELF

How You Express Yourself In Writing

Less than 50 points   This lower-than-average score would seem to indicate that you are not expressing yourself clearly when writing English. The closer your score to 50 points, the less serious this problem is likely to prove. Difficulties with written English are most frequently caused by inadequate learning early on in life; you could probably improve your performance considerably by taking some extra lessons. However, you should not assume that a below-average result means you are uneducated or unintelligent. Many people in high places in government, industry and science have difficulty writing clear, concise English. They sometimes fall into the trap of confusing long words and complex sentence-structure with profundity. Clarity in writing depends primarily on straight thinking rather than on an enormous vocabulary or great knowledge of the rules of syntax. Think out what you want to say, then set it down on paper with a maximum economy of expression. Only use words if they are the best ones for the job, and never put in two if just one will work as well.

Between 50 and 100 points

This is an average score-range which shows a reasonable aptitude for using written English clearly and exactly. The higher your score within this range, of course, the more proficient you are likely to prove when it comes to expressing your ideas in writing. If your early schooling in English was rather sketchy, then the level of natural aptitude revealed by this assessment probably means that you could increase your level of performance fairly quickly and easily. You appear to have a good 'feel' for the language and should master its more intricate rules without much effort.

More than 100 points

This score shows a true feeling for language and an excellent grasp of the rules of English usage. Such a result usually indicates both a sound schooling in writing technique and a natural aptitude for expressing oneself clearly and exactly. Being able to write good, concise English is an advantage in almost every occupation, even those in which success does not primarily depend on writing ability. For instance, a scientist, an engineer or a company director who can produce well-argued reports which express his ideas accurately yet clearly will be able to communicate far more effectively both with his own colleagues and with the general public. Your aptitude with words suggests that you might also be able to follow a career based on the ability to write, for instance as an editor, journalist, technical author or novelist. Whether your talents would be best directed into writing fiction or non-fiction depends on other abilities, such as powers of imagination and the capacity to absorb a large number of facts in a short amount of time. These mental skills have been explored elsewhere in the book; in the last chapter we will be showing you how to combine scores on the different assessments to construct an overall profile of your intellectual abilities.

ASSESSMENT NINE

HOW TO TAKE THIS TEST

The final assessment in this book differs from the others in two ways. First, the scoring system is slightly more complicated: you will be bringing together scores from four different areas of social behaviour to provide an in-depth analysis of your level of ability when relating to others. Second, unlike most of the items in previous assessments, there are no 'right' or 'wrong' answers; all we want you to do here is to identify those statements which come closest to reflecting your own attitudes, beliefs, feelings or responses to the situations described. There is no time limit; you should think carefully before answering, so that your replies truly correspond to your actual behaviour or thoughts. The greater the accuracy of your answers, the more reliable will be the resulting assessment of your socializing ability.

PART ONE

(1) I believe:
  (a) that it is not especially important to be on good terms with most of the people one meets.
  (b) that one should always make an effort to be on good terms with most of the people one meets.
  (c) that one should try very hard to be on good terms with everybody one meets.

(2) I find that the majority of people are:
  (a) unfriendly and hard to get to know.
  (b) usually friendly and easy to get along with.
  (c) almost always friendly and easy to get along with.

(3) When I am chatting to somebody socially, I tend to:
  (a) let them do most of the talking.

(b) share the conversation equally with them.

(c) do most of the talking myself.

(4) I find it difficult to relate to people from a different social or ethnic group:
  (a) most of the time.
  (b) now and then.
  (c) rarely or never.

(5) If a stranger smiled in my direction at a party, I would be most likely to:
  (a) become suspicious and wonder what his/her ulterior motive might be.
  (b) return the smile and think he/she was probably being friendly.
  (c) use it as an excuse to strike up a conversation.

(6) When talking to a friend:
  (a) I am careful not to let him/her know what I am really thinking.
  (b) I allow my feelings to show most of the time.
  (c) I always make my true feelings about an issue clear.

(7) If I am on my own for any length of time:
  (a) I am perfectly happy and rarely feel lonely.
  (b) I enjoy periods of solitude, provided they do not go on too long or occur too frequently.
  (c) I hate being on my own and will actively seek out the company of others, even that of strangers.

(8) If trapped by a boring guest at a party, I would:
  (a) be perfectly prepared to act rudely in order to get rid of them.
  (b) make a polite excuse to disengage from the conversation but, if that fails, stay there being bored.
  (c) put up with it for fear of upsetting them or hurting their feelings.

(9) When I am with other people at a party or similar social gathering:
  (a) I find myself getting bored fairly quickly and wishing I was elsewhere.
  (b) I enjoy myself most of the time I am there.
  (c) I love every minute of most parties and am sorry when they are over.

(10) (a) I have a wide circle of friends and get along well with people.
  (b) I have several friends and get along well with most people.
  (c) I have very few friends and find it hard to relate to others.

PART TWO

Here we want you to note down the truth or falsity of the following statements:

(1) I have a rich and varied social life. True/False

(2) When I invite people round, they often seem to have other engagements. True/False

(3) I am asked out, or invite friends around to my place, at least three times a month. True/False

(4) I would describe myself as a loner by nature. True/False

(5) I find it easy to get along with others. True/False

(6) I find the thought of going to parties makes me anxious. True/False

(7) I have a large circle of friends and acquaintances. True/False

(8) I feel isolated and lonely at present. True/False

(9) I am seldom at a loss for company in my free time. True/False

(10) When first introduced to somebody, I find it hard to know what to say. True/False

---

PART THREE

Note which statement below most accurately reflects your feelings in the situations described.

(1) When in conversation with somebody, I tend to:
 (a) talk a lot about my work because this is my main interest in life.
 (b) listen to what he/she has to say and occasionally make a comment.
 (c) allow the conversation to die, because I never know what to say next.

(2) If approached by a stranger at a party:
 (a) I welcome the chance to tell somebody new my jokes and stories.
 (b) I usually find it interesting to exchange views with somebody new.
 (c) I become anxious because I am unsure what is expected of me.

(3) To sustain a conversation, I will:
  (a) tell jokes to prevent silences from developing.
  (b) allow the exchange to flow without trying to direct it and not feel awkward about silences.
  (c) become embarrassed if the talk starts flagging and wonder desperately how to start a discussion going again.

(4) In conversations I tend to:
  (a) adopt a dominant role.
  (b) be neither especially dominant nor especially passive.
  (c) generally adopt a passive, listening role.

(5) When talking socially, my facial expression:
  (a) tends not to betray what I am really thinking.
  (b) mirrors my feelings.
  (c) may do either of the above, but I am not sure how I look when talking socially.

(6) If a person of the same sex puts an arm on my shoulder as we are talking, I:
  (a) try to move away, because such physical intimacy, even when non-sexual, upsets me.
  (b) respond without any feelings of embarrassment.
  (c) feel extremely uncomfortable but do not do anything for fear of hurting that person's feelings.

(7) When talking to somebody I tend to look him/her in the eyes:
  (a) much of the time.
  (b) now and then.
  (c) as little as possible.

(8) When meeting somebody for the first time, I am:
  (a) usually anxious to make the best possible impression.
  (b) not especially concerned about how I come across.
  (c) worried in case he/she forms a bad opinion of me.

(9) When talking to others, I use gestures to emphasize a point:
  (a) frequently.
  (b) now and then.
  (c) seldom or never.

(10) I tend to sum up other people:
  (a) very quickly, and then find little reason to change my opinions.
  (b) only after a few meetings, and very seldom after the first.
  (c) very quickly, only to find that my first impressions were wrong.

PART FOUR

Below, you will find ten pairs of words describing different social attributes. We want you to place yourself somewhere along the line between the two extremes by noting the letter closest to where you picture yourself on that particular dimension. For instance, in the first example, if you consider yourself a very friendly person, you might write down letter (A) or (B) as your answer. On the other hand, if you regard yourself as rather unfriendly, you would note down an (E) or even an (F).

Friendly (A)   (B)   (C)   (D)   (E)   (F) Unfriendly

Social (A)   (B)   (C)   (D)   (E)   (F) Unsociable

A good mixer (A)   (B)   (C)   (D)   (E)   (F) A loner

Attractive (A)   (B)   (C)   (D)   (E)   (F) Unattractive

Interesting to know (A) (B) (C) (D) (E) (F) Uninteresting to know

Loyal to friends (A)   (B)   (C)   (D)   (E)   (F) Disloyal to friends

Likeable (A)   (B)   (C)   (D)   (E)   (F) Unlikeable

Affectionate (A)   (B)   (C)   (D)   (E)   (F) Unaffectionate

Tolerant (A)   (B)   (C)   (D)   (E)   (F) Intolerant

Extravert (A)   (B)   (C)   (D)   (E)   (F) Introspective

HOW TO MARK THIS TEST

Part One

Give yourself **1 point** for each (a), **2 points** for every (b) and **3 points** for each (c) statement ticked. Make a note of this score.

Part Two

Give yourself **2 points** for every *odd*-number statement ticked as being *True*, and a further **2 points** for each *even*-number statement ticked as being *False*. No points can be awarded for *odd* statements marked as *False* or *even* statements ticked as *True*.

Part Three

Every (a) response gets **3 points**, each (b) **2 points** and the (c) statements **1 point** each. As in Part One, this gives a possible maximum of **30 points**. Now *add* this score to your score for Part One to produce a final score on these two portions of the assessment. Note the overall total separately.

Part Four

Give yourself **points** on the following basis: (A) = **5** (B) = **4** (C) = **3** (D) = **2** (E) = **1** (F) = **0**. This allows a possible maximum of **50** and a minimum of **0 points**. You should now *add* this score to the total obtained on Part Two to produce a final score on these two parts of this assessment.

My score for Parts One + Three =

My score for Parts Two + Four =

WHAT THIS TEST TELLS YOU ABOUT YOURSELF

You now have *two* different scores from this assessment: the total arrived at by adding together the scores on Parts One and Three, and that produced by adding the scores on Parts Two and Four. In order to discover how the various elements, which go to make up your level of social skills, combine, transfer those totals on to the chart below. The point on that table where the scores on Parts One and Three and those on Two and Four intersect directs you to a particular section below.

For example, suppose your scores on Parts One and Three added up to 43, while those on Parts Two and Four totalled 47. This would direct you to Section Five of the assessment. Equally, if your scores on Parts One and Three totalled 58, while the total on Parts Two and Four came to 65, you would be directed to Section One.

PARTS TWO + FOUR	PARTS ONE + THREE		
	More than 45	*Between 30 and 45*	*Less than 30*
More than 60	Section One	Section Four	Section Seven
Between 40 and 60	Section Two	Section Five	Section Eight
Less than 40	Section Three	Section Six	Section Nine

In the last chapter, when you come to assess your aptitudes for particular employment use this section number as your final score.

What The Scores Reveal

This assessment looked at several aspects of social aptitude and explored your ability to handle relationships and interact effectively with others in a number of different ways.

In the appropriate section below you will find an analysis of your social skills, together with some insights as to why, on occasions, you may find it hard to develop or sustain relationships.

Section One

This combination of scores suggests that you may be trying too hard to impress people and, on many occasions, failing to sustain a relationship because of this approach. You appear to have a good level of confidence in yourself and your ability to get along well with others, which should provide an excellent foundation on which to construct lasting and worthwhile friendships. You seem to be a very warm, if rather too dominant, individual who may not enjoy any situations over which you feel unable to exert a considerable degree of control. Because of this, you may tend to direct your social exchanges fairly forcefully and grow bored with them if the other person is unwilling to play a subordinate role. Perhaps you have too great a tendency to see people as a potential audience or as a means of keeping *you* from feeling bored, lonely or unloved. This may arise, to some extent, from a slight lack of assurance in your capacity to interest people in your own right. People who are extremely self-assured in most situations can still fear the consequences of relaxing their grip on events. Try to be more relaxed in all social situations, value people for themselves and allow *them* the opportunity to value *you* in the same way.

At work, if you are in a position of authority, be careful not to get the reputation of being something of a bore, or the sort of boss who is too overbearing. The fact that your subordinates may have to listen to you and show interest in or enthusiasm for the ideas you propose does not, of course, mean they are really attentive, interested or enthusiastic. The slight lack of self-assurance which may underline your approach is unlikely to be appreciated by those you seek to dominate and will make you more isolated than a less dominating, more relaxed superior.

If you are in a subordinate position, then your inability to control the direction of relationships at work may cause you certain anxiety. In your desire to remain at the centre of things you could develop the strategy of attempting to manipulate events behind the scenes. This approach is not calculated to make you popular with either your colleagues or, ultimately, your superiors.

Section Two

You have a reasonable level of self-esteem and assurance, being neither too positive nor too negative about your abilities and personality. It does, however, appear that you may on occasions be trying too hard to impress people. This may well result in relationships failing to develop as you would like them to, simply because others are put off by your overly forceful approach. Your need to dominate situations could stem from a basic lack of confidence in your ability to make friends and influence people simply by being yourself. Try to be more relaxed during social encounters, listen to other people and show a genuine interest in their views, rather than constantly trying to overwhelm them with the strength of your own personality.

At work, make certain that this need to dominate others does not make you too overbearing when in a position of power. People working for such a boss cannot relate to their superior in a way likely to promote an efficient and relaxed working environment.

As a subordinate, be careful that your need to control personal relationships does not cause you to try and manipulate events behind the scenes.

Section Three

You seem to have a rather negative sense of self-worth, which may be the reason why you attempt to dominate relationships. When somebody lacks self-assurance, it is very tempting to regard other people as a 'challenge' which must be confronted as forcefully as possible. This high-pressure approach, during which you try to take complete control of the social situation, is bound to put people off. They will feel uncertain how to respond and, if dominant themselves, are likely to resent your attempts to force them into a subordinate role. Do not be so critical of yourself. It is a mistake to focus on any negative aspects of your personality or appearance while failing to notice the equal number of positive features. Relax and be more natural in social encounters, learn to value people for themselves and get them to value you in the same way.

Be specially careful at work if you are in a position of authority. Your current approach to interpersonal relationships may make it very hard for you to cope with subordinates in a relaxed manner. You probably prefer to dominate discussions and exert a strong degree of control over other people's actions. It is also likely that you emphasize their faults, or their less attractive qualities, rather than being able to balance the good and bad points in those working under you.

If you are in a subordinate position yourself, then do not allow this rather negative self-attitude to undermine your confidence and prevent you from achieving your ambitions.

Section Four

This assessment suggests that you have a good deal of self-confidence, a positive sense of self-worth and a desire to enjoy a wide social life. In this you are probably reasonably successful, although you may find it hard to sustain some relationships which you would like to see endure. If you do have such a problem on occasions, a possible explanation could be that some people may see you as too confident, too self-assured and, perhaps, a trifle too arrogant. While it is very helpful to hold oneself in high regard, this can be a risky image to present to others, especially at a first meeting. If you try and sell your strong points too powerfully, others may be deterred from developing the relationship further or sustaining it over a prolonged period. Try to be more relaxed in your attitude to others and don't feel you need to impress them constantly with your positive features.

If you have authority at work, your social skills probably make you a popular superior most of the time. Be careful not to allow the tendency to appear rather too self-confident and assured on occasions make you seem arrogant.

However, if you are in a subordinate position, then resist the temptation to be very self-assured in front of an employer, especially one who is somewhat lacking in confidence. By doing so, you are likely to pose a threat to his own authority and status, and may find opportunities for advancement and promotion denied you as a result.

Section Five

The results of this assessment suggest that you have a realistic understanding of both your strong and weak points and enjoy a good social life. This is an ideal combination of scores and one which requires little further comment. If the statements were answered accurately, you appear to have an above-average level of social skills.

You are likely to prove an excellent employer who is able to exert authority and command respect without appearing either overbearing or arrogant. You are probably the kind of superior to whom subordinates bring their difficulties and problems, in the confident expectation of receiving a sympathetic hearing.

You have the skills to relate well to colleagues of equal status just as easily and effectively, while your superiors are likely to look on you favourably. Somebody with your level of social aptitude is ideally suited to any career that involves dealing with members of the public, smoothing out difficulties and solving interpersonal problems in the lives of others. You could, for instance, make a good doctor, nurse, psychologist or psychiatrist, an excellent teacher, social worker or public relations officer, an understanding lawyer or community relations official, an effective journalist or interviewer.

Section Six

From the assessment it appears that while you can get along with people reasonably well, and probably enjoy the company of others, you have a rather negative attitude towards your own good qualities. This may result in a certain lack of self-confidence in social situations which tends to detract from your overall performance. There may, for example, be occasions when you would like to make the first move in getting to know somebody better but be held back by such unhelpful thoughts as: 'I'll probably get a brush-off . . .', 'I'm not sufficiently attractive to interest somebody like that . . .', 'I don't suppose they would find me good company . . .' and so on. Concentrate more on your good points, the positive aspects of your personality and appearance, rather than allowing negative feelings to hold you back.

If you have a position of authority at work, do not allow this approach to undermine your confidence when dealing with colleagues or subordinates. It may be, because you lack the assurance to present your views and feelings directly, that you operate in what others might, perhaps rightly, regard as a somewhat devious fashion. Instead of making your true attitudes known directly, you either use somebody else to convey those opinions on your behalf or say one thing and actually believe and do another.

If you are a subordinate, do not allow this lack of social confidence to restrict your abilities and impede your opportunities of advancement by making you feel less positively than you should about your good qualities and abilities.

Section Seven

The assessment suggests that, while you are self-confident in some areas of your life, getting along with others poses problems which are most likely to arise in unstructured situations where you cannot be certain how they will respond. At a party or some other social gathering, for instance, you might be made anxious by having to meet strangers, and also experience difficulties over developing new friendships. These uncertainties are likely to be resolved, however, if you are in a situation where both your own behaviour and that of others in the relationship is to a large extent determined by the circumstances.

As an employer, a doctor, lawyer, or teacher for instance, you would probably have few difficulties in getting along with employees, patients, clients or students in the office, consulting-room or lecture hall. Outside these structured meetings, however, you could find it hard to feel relaxed and at ease. If you are in a subordinate position, then, again, getting along with colleagues or superiors while at work probably presents few problems, although you may well find it a good deal less easy to get along with them outside working hours.

Try to be more relaxed in your approach to socializing. Listen to others, rather than spending much of the time thinking about how *you* can best impress *them*. Develop a genuine interest in the people you meet socially, and value them for themselves rather than as an audience for your views or a safeguard against loneliness or boredom.

Section Eight

You appear to be having some difficulties in developing or sustaining social relationships or in knowing how best to handle other people. However, it also seems that you have a realistic and positive view of your own attributes and abilities and do not appear to try and dominate others. Part of your problem may be due to a rather too submissive attitude in your relationships; perhaps you are *too* concerned with making other people like you or be impressed by you. Although this sometimes makes it easier to develop friendships, such an approach may make it harder to sustain them. A reluctance to express one's true feelings, desires, needs and emotions leads to resentment by both parties, a sense of mutual distrust which can undermine the best relationship.

As a superior, you could find it hard to relate effectively to colleagues or subordinates, especially in situations where it becomes necessary to assert yourself and express views which are unpopular. People could come to regard you as somewhat two-faced, not because you want to deceive but because, by not saying or doing what you honestly feel should be said or done, you are prevented from taking action directly. Instead, you may prefer to work behind the scenes, placing the responsibility for the unpopular decisions you have to make on somebody else's shoulders.

As a subordinate, you may not stand up for yourself sufficiently, allowing more forceful colleagues to take advantage of your good nature and reluctance to do anything likely to make you unpopular. You may also find that others are reluctant to confide in you because you seem unwilling to express your own feelings, opinions and attitudes openly.

Try not to be so anxious about allowing people to see the real you. Attempts to impress, placate or buy friendship by always going along with what others want can be self-defeating. Have the confidence to expect people to value you for yourself and accept you on your own terms.

Section Nine

This assessment probably appears to confirm what you may have long believed, that you are unable to develop or sustain lasting relationships and have a low level of social skills. Although your scores would suggest that such a state of affairs exists at this moment, there is no real cause for despondency. The present situation has not arisen from an inborn inability to relate to others but only because, for some reason, your social skills have never been sufficiently developed. This can occur for a whole host of reasons, none of which is in any sense the *fault* of the individual concerned. For instance, an only child may find it harder to get along with people of his or her own age because, during the important formative years of infancy, they were relating to adults rather than to other children. Denied the necessary practice in childhood, their socializing aptitude remains at a low level. Similarly, children who are more intellectually advanced than their classmates may find it difficult to get along with them and so withdraw more and more into their studies. It often happens that these same children, later in life, go into professions or occupations that are more concerned with objects than with other people. At work, they can get along fine, because relationships in the clearly structured world of the professions present little difficulty. It is away from the office, the consulting-room and the laboratory that they find problems in relating to others.

It also appears from the assessment that you have a rather negative sense of your own competence and self-worth in regard to social skills. This lack of assurance in your ability to attract and hold the interest of other people is almost certainly misplaced. Even if your work is centred on manipulating things rather than dealing with people, it would pay you to acquire these skills. Start by coming to a more positive view of your own personality and attributes, make a resolution to develop a fuller social life and – while you are gaining more knowledge of and experience in social situations – watch the way other people cope with those situations which you currently find difficult.

To sum up

Why have we looked at social aptitude in this book? Being able to get along well with others is a skill on which the successful expression of other, more intellectual mental abilities so often crucially depends. These days, success in the majority of human activities demands the capacity for working as one of a team, being able to 'sell' your ideas to others, being able to attain the position in a company or profession that will allow you to translate your problem-solving talents and decision-making prowess into action.

Given an equal level of intellectual ability, it is almost always the person who is also socially skilled who achieves the most and attains desired goals in the shortest space of time. Indeed, somebody who is extremely gifted in this area may well make up for certain failings in other aspects of their mental performance and do better than intellectually more capable but socially less gifted men or women.

With all nine assessments scored, you are now in a position to bring together the knowledge which those assessments have provided, in order to determine the area of work for which you appear to possess the greatest aptitude.

YOUR HIDDEN TALENTS IN ACTION

When discussing the various aptitudes assessed by the nine tests in this book, we have considered the different occupations for which a particular talent would be especially suitable or entirely necessary. But, as we emphasized, it is usually essential to possess a combination of several aptitudes in order to succeed in most professions or occupations. The purpose of this final section is to reveal which collection of aptitudes appears most likely to lead to success in nearly 200 different careers. Some of these will be fairly obvious. It comes as no surprise, for example, to learn that a theoretical physicist needs an above-average talent for formal reasoning and scientific thinking. Nor is it in any way remarkable that successful doctors possess a considerable aptitude for social skills, what their patients would call 'a good bedside manner', in addition to a bent for scientific thinking. Other important aptitudes, however, will be less apparent, such as the clerical aptitude needed by a good teacher; the flair for languages required by a successful historian; the writing talent necessary in philosophy, or the high level of motor skills needed by members of the medical professions.

To compile the Careers Chart below, we administered our tests to men and women already in a wide range of professions and occupations. They were then asked to list those aptitudes which, in their opinion, would be either essential or very helpful towards success in their chosen careers. Finally we investigated their level of competence and attainment in a variety of ways. This assessment included talking to their colleagues, employers, superiors, students and so on; checking work records, publications in the scientific literature, sales of books or works of art, speed of promotion, and level of income. By comparing their actual scores with the idealized scores which they had produced and then relating these to the amount of success each volunteer had enjoyed in his or her chosen career, it was possible to produce an ideal score on each of the nine tests for every career analysed. Naturally, the criteria for assessing success varied considerably from one job to the next, but it always included a self-evaluation by the person concerned. We asked each individual how much he or she felt they had achieved; how much confidence they brought to their job; how much happiness their attainments had produced, and how much stimulation they found in their daily work.

Because our sample was fairly small in each case, the figures quoted on the

Careers Chart should be used only as a guide to the sort of aptitudes which seem most highly correlated to achievement in that particular occupation. We are constantly gathering further data for this study and, if you would like to help us in this task, we would be most grateful if you could complete the research form in the Appendix.

Because there is a considerable overlap of key aptitudes between certain professions and occupations, you will not find every possible career listed here. For example, since similar aptitudes are needed by a theoretical mathematician and a theoretical physicist, only the former has been listed. In almost every case, however, you can analyse the aptitudes relevant to an unlisted career by putting together those from related areas. Suppose, for instance, you are interested in finding out the talents necessary for success as a language teacher. You will find a general category of *Teacher (Arts)* in the Education portion of the Chart. In addition, you should look up the score for a successful *Interpreter* and/or a *Translator*. By combining the aptitudes under these different headings, you can obtain a clear idea of the demands made on your intellect by that particular job. Similarly, if you want to discover what aptitude you would need to possess as a translator of scientific papers, you could look under the appropriate heading in either the *Medicine* or *Science* categories of the Chart and combine these scores with those provided for *Translators*. Since the ability to write clearly is going to prove important, it would then be necessary to extract the aptitude scores found against the *Writer (Non-Fiction)* heading.

In those instances where different skills appeared to be needed for what, on the surface, might seem two very similar jobs, both occupations have been listed. Also, where we felt it would be hard to decide which career came closest to another, unlisted occupation, we included both. For this reason you will find that some of the listings have identical score patterns.

With a little thought, you should be able to discover the aptitudes associated with attainment in virtually any profession or occupation. This information can then be used in one of two different ways: either to decide whether you possess the right aptitudes for a career which you are currently following, or to discover which occupation would be best suited to your talents. In this way you can be guided towards the most appropriate choice of careers.

USING THE CHART

The occupations and professions are listed in alphabetical order under seventeen different categories which are, themselves, arranged alphabetically. These categories are: Administration; Agriculture; Arts and Crafts; Catering; Construction; Education; Entertainment; Financial; Law and Order; Media (Press, TV, etc.); Medicine; Military; Public Service; Scientific; Sports (Professionals); Transport; and finally Miscellaneous.

To use the Chart, take a sheet of plain paper and place it along the line marked *Your Own Scores on Tests*. Note down your scores, under each of the assessment numbers (see below) on the sheet of paper. Take care to ensure that your scores are placed under each of the numbered boxes, since this will make it easier to match them with those listed.

Now refer to the occupation or profession of interest, or the combination of aptitudes necessary to produce a profile of the career you have in mind. Place the sheet of paper containing your own score along the line beneath the printed scores and compare them. If a particular aptitude is neither helpful nor unhelpful in a certain job then the box will contain a cross. When this happens, you should ignore your score under that assessment heading.

In order to ensure that you have the aptitudes needed to find fulfilment and attain success in a chosen career, *your scores should be equal to or greater than those listed*. If they are somewhat lower on just one of the aptitudes, then you might still be capable of tackling that career successfully. If they are all well below those on the chart, then you should seriously consider whether such an occupation would prove to be the most rewarding one for you.

The assessments are listed on the chart in the order they were presented in this book:

> (1) Perceptual Processing Aptitude
> (2) Language Aptitude
> (3) Scientific Thinking Aptitude
> (4) Creative Thinking Aptitude
> (5) Formal Reasoning Aptitude
> (6) Hand/Eye Co-ordination Aptitude
> (7) Artistic Aptitude
> (8) Writing Aptitude
> (9) Social Aptitude

Key: L = below average   A = average   H = above average
     FA = fast-accurate   SA = slow-accurate   + = disregard

Assessment number	1	2	3	4	5	6	7	8	9
Your own scores on tests									
Administration									
Clerical Assistant	FA	+	A	+	+	+	+	A	A
Company Director	FA/SA	A	A	H	A	+	+	H	H
Company Secretary	+	+	H	+	+	+	+	H	A
Interpreter	FA	H	+	+	+	+	+	H	A
Office Manager	FA/SA	+	+	+	+	+	+	H	H
Secretary	FA	+	+	+	+	FA	+	A	A
Storekeeper	FA/SA	+	+	+	+	+	+	A	H
Switchboard Operator	FA	+	+	+	+	FA	+	+	A
Transport Manager	FA/SA	+	+	+	+	+	+	A	A
Agriculture									
Cat/Dog Breeder	+	+	A	+	+	FA/SA	+	A	+
Estate/Farm Manager	FA/SA	+	+	+	+	+	+	H	H
Farmer	+	+	A	A	+	FA/SA	+	+	+
Forester	+	+	A	+	+	FA/SA	+	+	+
Gardener	+	+	A	A	+	SA	A	+	+
Horticulturalist	+	+	H	A	+	SA	A	A	+
Landscape Gardener	+	+	+	H	+	SA	H	+	+
Veterinarian	+	+	H	A	+	FA	+	A	H
Arts/Crafts									
Bookbinder	SA	+	+	+	+	SA	+	+	+
Embroiderer	+	+	+	H	+	FA	H	+	+
Graphic Designer	SA/FA	+	+	H	+	FA/SA	H	+	A
Lithographer	SA/FA	+	+	A	+	FA/SA	A	+	+
Model Maker	+	+	+	H	+	FA/SA	A	+	+
Painter	+	+	+	H	+	FA	H	+	+
Photographer	FA/SA	+	A	H	+	FA	H	+	H
Photographic Printer	FA/SA	+	A	A	+	FA/SA	A	+	A
Picture Restorer	+	+	+	A	+	SA	A	+	+
Potter	+	+	+	H	+	FA	H	+	+
Sculptor	+	+	+	H	+	SA	H	+	+
Silversmith/ Goldsmith	+	+	+	H	+	SA	H	+	+
Watchmaker	FA/SA	+	+	+	+	SA	+	+	A

Assessment number	1	2	3	4	5	6	7	8	9
Catering									
Chef	FA/SA	+	+	H	+	FA	A	+	A
Hotel Manager	FA	A	+	+	+	+	+	A	H
Hotel Receptionist	FA/SA	+	+	+	+	+	+	A	H
Publican/Barman	FA/SA	+	+	+	+	FA/SA	+	+	H
Restaurateur	FA	A	+	+	+	FA/SA	+	+	H
Waiter	+	+	+	+	+	FA	+	+	H
Construction									
Architect	FA/SA	+	A	H	A	FA/SA	H	A	A
Bricklayer	+	+	+	+	+	SA	A	+	A
Carpenter	FA/SA	+	+	+	+	FA/SA	+	+	A
Decorator	FA/SA	+	+	A	+	FA/SA	A	+	A
Electrical Engineer	FA/SA	+	A	A	H	FA/SA	+	A	A
Engineer (Mechanical)	FA/SA	+	A	A	H	FA/SA	+	A	A
Planning Officer	FA	+	+	+	A	+	+	H	A
Plumber	+	+	+	+	+	SA	+	+	A
Surveyor	SA/FA	+	+	+	A	SA	+	A	A
Education									
Careers Adviser	FA	+	+	A	+	+	+	H	H
Educational Psychologist	FA/SA	A	H	A	+	+	+	H	H
Infants Teacher	+	+	+	+	+	+	+	A	H
Librarian	FA	A	+	+	+	FA/SA	+	H	H
Principal	FA/SA	A	A	+	+	+	+	H	H
Remedial Teacher	FA/SA	A	A	H	+	FA/SA	A	H	H
School Secretary	FA	A	+	+	+	FA/SA	+	A	H
Teacher (Arts)	FA/SA	+	+	H	+	FA/SA	H	H	H
Teacher (Science)	FA/SA	A	H	A	H	FA/SA	+	H	H
Teacher (Sports)	FA/SA	+	+	+	+	FA	+	A	H
University Lecturer	FA/SA	A	A	A	A	+	A	H	H
Entertainment									
Actor/Actress	+	+	+	A	+	+	+	+	H
Comedian/Comedienne	+	+	+	H	+	+	+	+	H
Conjurer	+	+	+	A	+	FA	+	+	H
Dancer	+	+	+	A	+	FA	+	+	A
Film Director	FA/SA	+	+	H	+	+	A	H	H
Make-up Artist	+	+	+	H	+	FA	H	+	A
Mime	+	+	+	H	+	SA	A	+	A
Musician	FA	+	+	A	+	FA	+	+	A
Producer (Films)	FA/SA	+	+	A	+	+	A	A	H
Producer (Stage)	FA/SA	+	+	A	+	+	H	A	H

Assessment number	1	2	3	4	5	6	7	8	9
Set Designer	+	+	+	H	+	SA	H	A	A
Singer	+	+	+	H	+	+	+	+	H
Stage Manager	FA/SA	+	+	A	+	SA/FA	A	+	H
Stunt-Person	+	+	+	A	+	FA	A	+	A
Television Announcer	FA/SA	A	+	A	+	+	+	A	H
Television Cameraman	FA	+	+	H	+	FA	H	+	+

Financial

	1	2	3	4	5	6	7	8	9
Accountant	FA	+	A	+	A	+	+	H	A
Actuary	+	+	H	+	H	+	+	H	A
Bank Manager	FA	+	A	A	+	+	+	H	A
Book-keeper	FA	+	+	+	+	+	+	A	A
Economist	FA/SA	+	H	A	H	+	+	H	+
Financial Consultant	FA/SA	+	H	A	A	+	+	H	H
Insurance Underwriter	FA	+	A	A	A	+	+	H	A
Mortgage Broker	FA/SA	+	+	+	+	+	+	A	A
Property Developer	+	+	A	A	+	+	A	A	A
Stockbroker	FA	+	A	+	+	+	+	A	A

Law and Order

	1	2	3	4	5	6	7	8	9
Criminal Lawyer	FA/SA	+	H	H	+	+	+	H	A
Criminologist	FA/SA	A	H	A	A	+	+	H	+
Customs Officer	FA	A	+	+	+	+	+	A	A
Detective (Police)	FA/SA	+	+	+	+	+	+	A	H
Detective (Private)	FA/SA	+	A	A	+	+	+	A	A
Forensic Scientist	FA	+	A	A	A	SA	+	H	+
Intelligence Officer	FA	A	A	A	+	+	+	H	+
Lawyer (Civil)	FA	+	H	A	+	+	+	H	A
Lawyer (Barrister)	FA	+	H	H	+	+	+	H	H
Legal Executive	FA/SA	+	A	A	+	+	+	H	A
Magistrate	FA/SA	+	+	A	+	+	+	A	A
Police Officer	FA/SA	+	+	+	+	+	+	A	H
Prison Governor	FA/SA	+	+	+	+	+	+	A	A
Probation Officer	FA	+	+	A	+	+	+	H	H

Media (Press/TV etc.)

	1	2	3	4	5	6	7	8	9
Advertising Copy Writer	+	+	+	H	+	+	A	H	A
Broadcaster	FA/SA	A	+	A	+	+	+	A	H
Editor	FA	A	A	A	+	+	A	H	A
Journalist	FA/SA	A	A	H	+	+	+	H	H
Publisher	FA	A	A	A	+	+	A	A	A
Sub-Editor	FA	+	+	A	+	+	A	H	+
Typographer	FA	+	+	+	+	FA	A	+	+
Writer (Fiction)	+	+	+	H	+	+	+	H	+
Writer (Non-Fiction)	FA/SA	A	A	A	+	+	+	H	A

Assessment number	1	2	3	4	5	6	7	8	9
Medicine									
Clinical Psychologist	FA/SA	+	H	A	+	+	+	H	H
Doctor	FA/SA	+	A	A	+	FA	+	A	H
Eye-Surgeon	FA/SA	+	H	A	+	FA	+	A	A
Laboratory Technician	FA	+	A	+	+	FA/SA	+	A	+
Mechanic (Dental)	FA/SA	+	+	+	+	FA	+	+	+
Medical Researcher	FA	+	H	H	+	FA/SA	+	H	+
Medical Secretary	FA	+	+	+	+	FA	+	H	A
Midwife	+	+	A	+	+	FA	+	+	H
Nurse	FA	+	A	+	+	FA	+	+	H
Optician	FA	+	A	A	+	FA/SA	+	+	A
Osteopath	+	+	A	A	+	FA	+	+	A
Pathologist	FA/SA	+	A	+	+	FA/SA	+	H	+
Pharmacist	FA	A	A	+	+	FA	+	A	A
Physiotherapist	+	+	+	A	+	FA	+	+	A
Psychiatrist	FA/SA	+	A	H	+	+	+	H	H
Psychologist (Clinical)	FA/SA	+	H	H	+	+	+	H	H
Radiographer	FA	+	A	+	+	FA	+	+	A
Surgeon (Dental)	FA/SA	+	+	A	+	FA	A	A	A
Surgeon (General)	FA/SA	+	A	A	+	FA	+	A	A
Military									
Bomb Disposal Officer	FA/SA	+	+	+	+	FA	+	+	+
Defence Analyst	FA/SA	A	H	A	+	+	+	H	A
Fighter Pilot	+	+	+	+	+	FA	+	+	+
Helicopter Pilot	+	+	+	+	+	FA	+	+	+
Military Strategist	FA	+	A	H	+	+	+	A	+
Naval Commander	FA	+	+	A	+	+	+	+	A
Officer (Army)	FA	+	+	+	+	+	+	+	A
Quartermaster	FA	+	+	+	+	+	+	A	+
Radar Operator	FA	+	A	+	+	FA	+	+	+
Public Service									
Antique Dealer	FA/SA	+	+	+	+	+	A	+	A
Auctioneer	FA/SA	+	+	A	+	+	+	+	A
Beautician	+	+	+	A	+	FA	A	+	H
Debt Collector	FA	+	+	A	+	+	+	A	H
Fireman	FA/SA	+	+	+	+	FA	+	+	A
Garage Mechanic	+	+	+	A	+	FA/SA	+	+	A
Hairdresser	+	+	+	+	H	FA/SA	H	+	H
Income-Tax Inspector	FA	+	A	+	A	+	+	H	H

Assessment number	1	2	3	4	5	6	7	8	9
Marriage-Guidance Expert	FA/SA	+	+	H	+	+	+	H	H
Minister of Religion	+	+	+	A	+	+	+	A	H
Politician	+	+	+	H	+	+	+	A	H
Public Relations Person	+	+	+	H	+	+	A	H	H
Salesman (Estate)	+	+	+	H	+	+	+	A	H
Shop Assistant	FA/SA	+	+	+	+	+	+	+	H
Social Worker	FA/SA	A	+	A	+	+	+	H	H
Undertaker	+	+	+	A	+	+	A	+	H
Scientific									
Anthropologist	+	H	H	H	+	+	+	H	+
Archaeologist	+	A	A	A	+	+	A	H	A
Biologist	FA/SA	+	H	H	A	FA/SA	+	H	+
Chemist	FA/SA	+	H	H	H	FA	+	H	+
Computer Programmer	FA	A	+	H	H	+	+	+	+
Geologist	+	+	H	A	+	FA	+	H	+
Metallurgist	FA/SA	+	H	A	H	FA/SA	+	A	+
Nuclear Physicist	FA/SA	+	H	H	H	+	+	H	+
Philosopher	+	A	H	H	+	+	A	H	+
Psychologist (Research)	FA/SA	+	H	H	A	+	+	H	A
Statistician	FA/SA	+	H	A	H	+	+	A	+
Theoretical Mathematician	FA/SA	+	H	H	H	+	+	H	P
Sports (Professionals)									
Chess Player	FA	+	A	H	H	+	+	+	+
Golfer	+	+	+	A	+	FA/SA	+	+	+
Gymnast	+	+	+	A	+	FA	A	+	+
Poker Player	FA	+	A	H	+	+	+	+	H
Racing Driver	+	+	+	A	+	FA	+	+	A
Tennis/Squash Player	FA	+	+	H	+	FA	+	+	+
Transport									
Airline Pilot	FA	+	+	A	A	FA	+	+	A
Air Traffic Controller	FA	+	+	A	+	FA	+	+	A
Bus Driver	+	+	+	+	+	FA	+	+	A
Engine Driver	FA/SA	+	+	+	+	FA	+	+	+
Navigation Officer	FA	+	+	+	A	+	+	+	A
Taxi Driver	+	+	+	+	+	FA	+	+	H

We began this book by explaining that self-knowledge was probably the most powerful piece of information anybody could hope to acquire. If you completed the assessments correctly, you will now be in possession of just such knowledge: an objective understanding of your intellectual strengths and weaknesses. This insight into your hidden talents, this understanding of your true aptitudes, makes it possible to choose wisely and well when coming to a decision about a career, a course of study or a leisure activity.

The fact that you possess those aptitudes essential to success in a particular activity does not, of course, mean that you will inevitably be successful, since there are other factors, such as motivation, self-image, attitudes and anxiety, which exert considerable influence over attainments. Nor can one exclude the part played by chance or personal feelings on the part of others; the lucky break and the unexpected setback; the promotion that takes no account of personal worth and the change in circumstances which offers previously undreamed-of opportunities for advancement.

With the knowledge now at your disposal, however, it should be possible to control many of these variables far more effectively. Select a career based on your true aptitudes, and it is almost certain that your motivation will be powerful and your self-image strong. Your attitudes will be sufficiently positive to respond to challenge, while your anxiety will be reduced in the face of difficulties because you now understand your mental strengths so much better than most. Because of this, you should find it easier to act on the lucky break, ride out surprise storms, exploit opportunities and not become overly depressed by setbacks.

A story about the famous British barrister F. E. Smith perfectly summarizes the position we hope you find yourself in at the end of this book. On one occasion he made a very long, very detailed and extremely brilliant submission in law. He talked with great eloquence for many hours, the table before him stacked with every kind of learned tome and legal volume. Finally he completed his flawless exposition and sat down.

The judge considered for a few moments, then said with a sigh: 'I very much fear, Mr Smith, after all that I am none the wiser.'

'No wiser, I accept, My Lord,' replied the barrister, 'but infinitely better informed!'

Knowing your own mind may not make you any wiser, but it does make you better informed about your untapped talents. Putting that knowledge to practical use is not only the first step towards success; it is also an act of true wisdom.

RESEARCH FORM

If you are willing to help us in our research, please complete the details below. To avoid spoiling the book, this page should either be copied or photocopied.

All information will be treated in strict confidence. Please return the completed form to: David Lewis, 22 Queen Anne Street, London W1.

Your Name .... (Dr,Mr,Mrs,Ms)
Your Address .... *Date of birth*
....
Your Occupation ....

Assessment Number	1	2	3	4	5	6	7	8	9
Your Assessment Scores	□	□	□	□	□	□	□	□	□

How Long in Present Job? ....

On a scale of 0–10 (where 0 = none at all, 5 = average amount, and 10 = complete), please assess the following:

How much stimulation do you find in your current work? ....
How much success do you consider you have enjoyed in your work? ....
How much happiness does your work give you? ....

If you had the chance to change your career now, would you do so? YES/NO.
If YES, what occupation would you sooner follow? ....

Please tick the aptitudes below on which you would expect somebody who is successful in your present work to obtain an above-average score.

(1) Perceptual Processing
(2) Language
(3) Scientific Thinking
(4) Creative Thinking
(5) Formal Reasoning
(6) Hand/Eye Co-ordination
(7) Artistic
(8) Writing
(9) Social

Did your results on these assessments surprise you? YES/NO.
If YES, what aptitude do you (or do you not) appear to possess that surprised you?
I do possess .... I do not possess ....

INDEX

abilities, 8–9
  artistic, 100, 106–7
  choice of occupation, 132–40
  divergent thinking, 63–8
  formal reasoning, 79–82
  hand/eye co-ordination, 90–92
  language learning, 37–41
  scientific thinking, 52–4
  social skills, 125–31
  speed and accuaracy, 26–30
  writing, 117–19
abstract symbols, 80
accuracy and speed, 26–30
administrative careers, 135
advertising, 28, 63, 137
agriculture, 135
air traffic control, 28
analysis, 52–4
applied mathematics, 81
aptitudes, 8–9
  choice of occupation, 132–40
  see also abilities
Arabic language, 39, 41
Armstrong, Richard, 100
artistic ability, 7, 100, 106–7
arts, 63–4, 135

Brady, Matthew, 106–7
Bulgarian language, 39
Burrows, Larry, 106

Capa, Robert, 106
careers chart, 132–40
catering, 136
chess, 79, 82
Chinese language, 39, 40
'clerical aptitude', 26
clerical work, 27

composition, artistic ability, 100, 106–7
computer operators, 27–8
computer programming, 81–2
concentration, 92
confidence, 126–31
construction industry, 29, 136
content validity, 37
convergent thinking, 63, 66–7
co-ordination, 7, 90–92
crafts, 29, 91, 106, 135
craftsmanship, 92
creativity, 52, 54, 63–8
Czech language, 39, 41

Danish language, 39
decorating, 29
deduction, scientific, 7
design sense, 100, 106–7
divergent thinking, 63–8
draughts (board game), 79, 82
drawing, 106
Dutch language, 39

education, 137
Einstein, Albert, 53, 64
English language, writing ability,
  117–19
entertainment industry, 136–7
evaluation, scientific thinking, 53
evening classes, 8
experimental work, 53–4
expression, power of, 7
eye/hand co-ordination, 90–92

Farsi language, 39
fast-accurate performers, 90–91
fast-accurate thinkers, 26–8, 30
financial world, 28, 137

Finnish language, 39, 40, 41
flow-charts, 65
fluency of thought, 64
formal reasoning, 79–82
French language, 39, 41
friendships, 126–31

games, formal reasoning, 82
German language, 39, 40
grammar, 38
graphic design, 106
Greek language (modern), 39, 40, 41
Gulf-State languages, 39

hand/eye co-ordination, 90–92
heraldry, 106
Hilbert, David, 80
hobbies, 8
    artistic ability, 106
    formal reasoning, 82
    hand/eye co-ordination, 91, 92
    slow-accurate thinkers, 30
horticulture, 29
Hungarian language, 39, 40

illustrating, 106
imaginative thinking, 63–8
Indo-European languages, 39
inspiration, 53
insurance underwriting, 54
interior decorating, 107
intuition, 53
Italian language, 39, 41

Japanese language, 39, 40
journalism, 28, 119, 137

languages, 7
    aptitude, 37–41
    choice of, 39–41
    computer, 81–2
    and creative thought, 66
    linguistic associations, 65–6
    writing ability, 117–19
Latin language, 39
legal work, 29, 137

leisure activities, 8
    artistic ability, 106, 107
    fast-accurate thinkers, 28
    formal reasoning, 82
    hand/eye co-ordination, 91, 92
    slow-accurate thinkers, 30
librarianship, 29
linguistic associations, 65–6
linguistic particles, 40
literature, 63, 64, 119
logical thought, 7, 52–4

magic, 91
manual tasks, hand/eye co-ordination,
    90–92
mathematics, 79, 80–81
media, 28, 137
medicine, 29, 138
memory, working, 37–8
mental images, 66
military careers, 138
model-making, 91, 92
music, 63, 64, 91

Norwegian language, 39

objectivity, 53, 54
occupation, choice of, 132–40
office work, 26, 27
Oriental languages, 39, 40

painting, 63–4, 91, 92, 106
perceptual processing, 26
photography, 106–7
Picasso, Pablo, 64
poetry, 64
Polish language, 39, 41
Portuguese language, 39
printing industry, 106
profession, choice of, 132–40
public service careers, 138–9
publishing, 28
punch-card operators, 27–8

radar operators, 28
radio, careers in, 28

reading ability, 26
reasoning ability, 52–4
  formal reasoning, 79–82
  logical reasoning, 7, 52–4
relationships, social skills, 125–31
research, 53
Romance languages, 39
Russian language, 39–40, 41

science, 29, 139
scientific thinking, 52–4
self-assurance, 126–7, 128
self-confidence, 126–31
self-esteem, 127
sentence-structure, 40
Serbo-Croatian language, 39
Slavic languages, 39–40, 41
slow-accurate performers, 90, 92
slow-accurate thinkers, 26, 28–30
Smith, Eugene, 106
Smith, F. E., 142
social skills, 7, 125–31
Spanish language, 39, 40, 41

speed and accuracy, 26–30
sport, careers in, 139
  fast-accurate thinkers, 28
  slow-accurate thinkers, 30
Swedish language, 39
symbols, formal reasoning, 79–82
syntax, 38

technology, 27–8, 81
television careers, 28, 136–7
Teutonic languages, 39
Torrance, Dr E., 64
transport careers, 139

Ural-Altaic languages, 39

vocabulary, 38, 41, 65–6

word-order, 40
working memory, 37–8
writing, ability, 117–19
  creative, 63, 64